I Touched God

The Loving Light Books Series

Book 1: God Spoke through Me to Tell You to Speak to Him
Book 2 & 3: No One Will Listen to God & You are God
Book 4: The Sun and Beyond
Book 5: The Neverending Love of God
Book 6: The Survival of Love
Book 7: We All Go Together
Book 8: God's Imagination
Book 9: Forever God
Book 10: See the Light
Book 11: Your Life as God
Book 12: God Lives
Book 13: The Realization of Creation
Book 14: Illumination
Book 15: I Touched God
Book 16: I and God are One
Book 17: We All Walk Together
Book 18: Love Conquers All
Book 19: Come to the Light of Love
Book 20: The Grace is Ours

Also by Liane Rich

The Book of Love
For the Love of God: An Introduction to God
For the Love of Money: Creating Your Personal Reality
Your Individual Divinity: Existing in Parallel Realities
For the Love of Life on Earth
Your Return to the Light of Love: a guidebook to spiritual awakening

Loving Light

Book 15

I Touched God

Liane Rich

The information contained in this book is not intended as a substitute for professional medical advice. Neither the publisher nor the author is engaged in rendering professional advice to the reader. The remedies and suggestions in this book should not be taken, or construed, as standard medical diagnosis, prescription or treatment. For any medical issue or illness consult a qualified physician.

Loving Light Books

ISBN 13: 978-1-878480-15-6
ISBN 10: 1-878480-15-4

Loving Light Books:
www.lovinglightbooks.com

Also Available at:
Amazon: www.amazon.com
Barnes & Noble: www.barnesandnoble.com

for Buffie

The information in this series is not necessarily meant to be taken literally. It is meant to *shift* your consciousness....

Foreword

Anyone immersed in the vast body of new metaphysical knowledge is aware of the virtual symphony of voices from channeled sources throughout the world – inspirational voices that may be artistic, poetic, philosophical, religious, or scientific. And now, out of these myriad New Age voices, comes a series of books by God, channeled through Liane, revealing the frank truth in all its glory and wonder, telling us how to cleanse our bodies, gain access to our subconscious minds, clear our other selves and march back to who we are – God.

In God's books you will be introduced to a loving, powerful, gripping, exciting, and often humorous voice that reaches out and speaks ever so personally to the individual reader. As the reader's interest deepens, invariably an intimate relationship to this voice develops. It is a relationship that lasts forever, and I am quite certain I do mean forever.

Here is an accelerated program, a no-holds-barred course, where God guides us and loves us, and as needs be recommends books to us and even a movie or musical piece along the way. He (She) enters our lives and sees through our eyes, seeming to enjoy the ride as He guides us back to US, back to ALL. Here is a voice that is playful and informative, that is humorous and serious, that is gentle and powerfully divine. It is a voice that knows no barriers or restrictions, a straightforward and honest voice that caresses us when we need the warmth and pushes us when we are immobilized.

In today's New Age literature there is an avalanche of information from magnificent beings of light, information that possesses us and compels us to look at our fears and express our love. In this series of books by God, you will find truly powerful methods for making this transition from toxicity to purity, from density to light, from fear to love, and from the delusion of death to the awakening to full life. You will experience in these books the love and the power of God for it is your love to express and your power to behold. Rarely will you see more lucid steps for transformation. Read these beautiful words and rejoice in our period of awakening, our return to Home.

John Farrell, PhD., LCSW. – Psychologist, Clinical Social Worker, Senior Clinician Psychiatric Emergency Services, U.C. Davis Medical Center, Sacramento. John is also a retired Professor – California State University, Sacramento, in Health Sciences and Psychology.

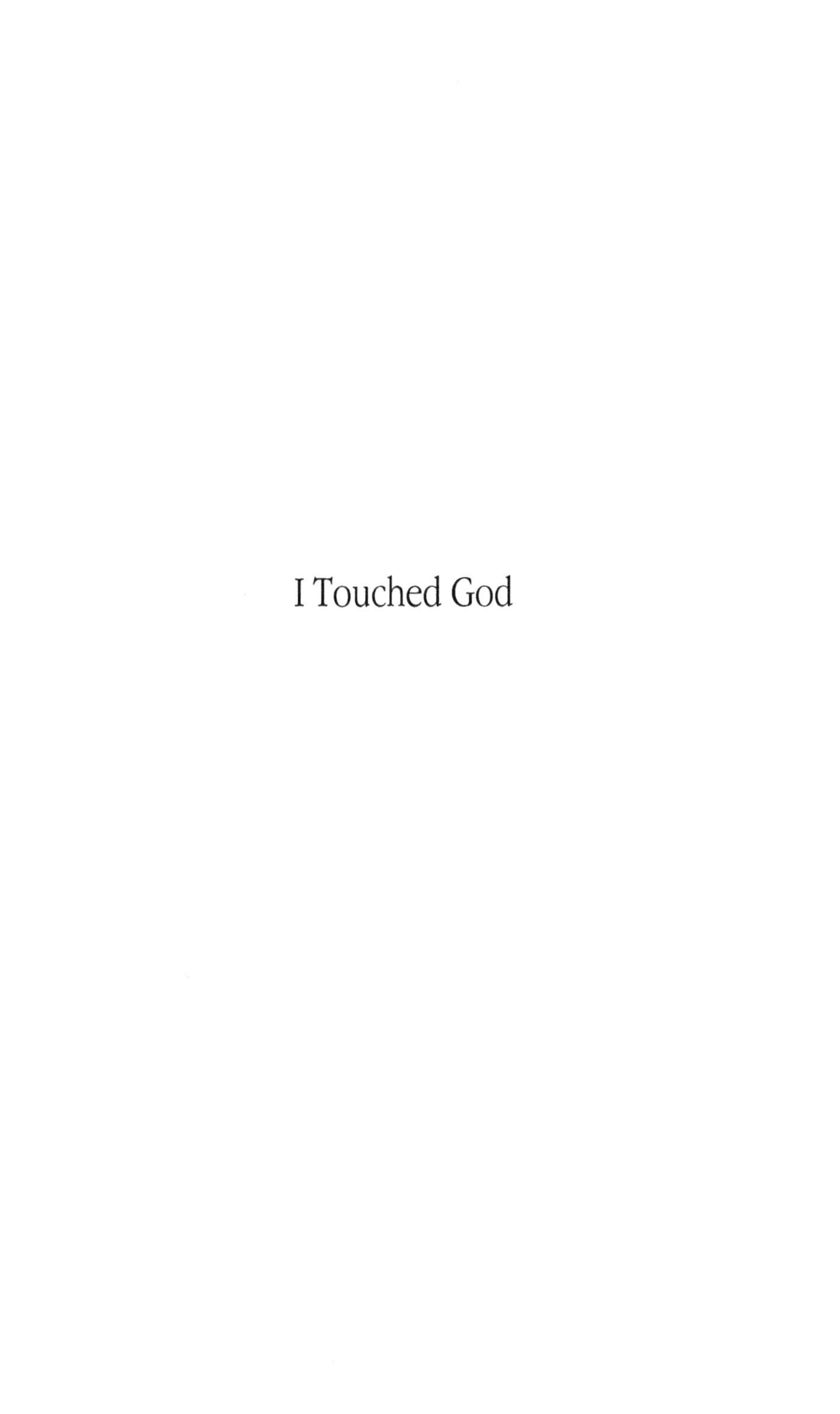

I Touched God

You have become so fearful that you no longer know how to decide what you really want. You do not trust you enough to allow you to make certain choices and you are afraid that you will choose as you have in the past and create greater problems for yourself. You do not trust you and you do not trust God. So, who do you trust? There is no one for you to trust and so you move without trust. You simply allow this or that to occur and you hope for the best. When you finally learn that you are God, you will wish to know that you have always been in a certain amount of trust concerning yourself. You know on some levels that you are God, and those who know have trust that God is in charge and everything is just fine.

You will find that, as you begin to become more aware of all parts of you, you will become more trustful of you. This is a natural evolution and it will take a little time once you open the door that is connected to your higher understanding. Many of you do not wish to be put in a situation of not knowing what tomorrow will bring, and so you will refuse to move forward unless you have been spoon fed information that will allow you to trust. Others have already developed a sense of adventure and will willingly and sometimes trustingly move into their future.

Do not be afraid to move out on your own. You need not wait for everyone else to catch on before you move ahead. Be ready to do what is best for you and do not be so concerned with those who wish you to stay in safe waters. You will always have those who are more afraid and always those who are less afraid. Fear is divided into degrees and what frightens you may not frighten your neighbor.

When you begin to see how you may move freely and gently without causing struggle and pain, you will wish to move and flow into your future. It was never necessary for pain to play a part but, somehow, you began to believe it would be a good idea to have a "signal" to let you know when you were off track. Now pain is common and you do not know how to send yourself clues about how you are developing without it. You even call some pain "growing pains." So, how do we begin to wean you off of pain and onto trust? You will find that trust will show you a much smoother ride and trust will allow you to be all that you can be. You will no longer fear punishment because you will no longer be *using* pain to guide you. You will be using trust to guide you, and you will be allowing God to come into you and to share your life with you.

When you begin to *live in trust*, you will begin to see because you will be *in the light*. As you move from pain to trust, you will wobble back and forth for some time, and then you will find your balance in trust and you will simply sit back and relax and allow God to drive you around. When you reach this point you will literally have chosen God over pain and you will literally have reached into you to unveil your trust. Your trust is very powerful. Your trust in God is probably your most valuable possession. Without trust in God you remain outside of God by choice. Not that anyone can be outside of God, but in refusing to acknowledge God you refuse to allow God to be part of you. Not that anyone can 'not' be part of God. Everyone is God, but in refusing to acknowledge God you can pretend forever whatever you want to pretend, and you will continue to live in your pretend world that you have created without your belief that God is you. And in this pretend world you may become many things and have trust in whatever you choose.

It is best to put your trust in God! God is in you and God is already here. He/she has always been and always will be so he/she is a pretty good bet... that is if you're looking for someone who will never leave and someone who has been around awhile and knows the ins and outs. Who would you rather put your faith in? Is it safer to believe in pain that will signal you when you get off track or is it easier to say, "God, you drive I'm going to rest for a while. I'm going to finally put down my guard and let someone else ride shotgun over my life. I'm going to even close my eyes and *trust* you to take me wherever you think is best. I trust you God. Would you be my partner and stay to take real good care of me?" And when you ask, God will drive and watch over you and take real good care of you. And when you hit a bump in the road do not wake up from your nap and start blaming God.

There are still bumps in the road but God is with you now. He knows where to take you and how to get there. You may not recognize the terrain because you have not been home in a very long time. God knows where you came from and where you are going. Do you? Do you know enough to take the wheel away from God because the road is bumpy? I think you will wish to reconsider.

So, now that you are finally allowing God to drive you home how will you handle it? Will you tell him how to drive, when to go faster, when to slow down, or will you simply allow God to be in charge? It's up to you, you know? You can allow God to be in charge or you can reclaim your control at any given moment. I suggest that you give up your control and all your rights. I know you don't like the sounds of this, but it is what I suggest. Let go of your rights and only remind yourself that God is driving you home and he knows where home is. Will your need for rights get you home? No. I do not think so.

Now you are in the car and God is personally driving you to your destination. You may rest now, or you may watch in wonder as you see where he is taking you, or you may simply read a good book, or turn on the radio and sing a song for God. Not too loud though. God has very sensitive ears. As a matter of fact God knows without hearing so you need never ask. You need only "know" that what you want is God. Most of you do not trust what you want because, sometimes, when you get what you want you get trouble too. So, stop wanting situations and things and gifts and start wanting God. God is the greatest gift and God is not only the greatest gift – God is you. When you want you, you will have come home to *love.*

⁂

You will find that as you begin to grow in trust you will be very well taken care of. The more you trust the more you create from trust. As this cycle continues you will be building on trust. Trust will be the foundation of your life. Once you receive trust you will be unable to return to fear. Trust is so strong that it is capable of wiping out your need for fear. Yes, fear is a need in you as is love and desire. Fear is a need that is regularly fulfilled by your requests. These requests are quite common as the need for fear is great.

Once you learn to do without fear you will be learning to rise above the world of pain. Pain and fear are connected. You usually fear that "this or that" will hurt you or cause you harm in some way, and so the fear of pain is associated with the degree of pain you might receive. You continually program yourself to receive pain by pushing your fear. You push your fear as far as you can because you do not like fear. It does not feel good to you so you try to shut it off and push it deep into you. Begin to admit that you have fear and to feel your fear. Begin to go into your fearful feelings in order to raise them up. Be in your fear. Feel it. Enjoy exploring it until it dissolves. Fear is just a feeling and it robs you of all other feelings. Fear is so strong that it can take your breath away... literally. Some have even been frightened to death. Their heart stops and they die of fear or fright.

You will not find fear in your ascended state. Fear is a very dense, humorless feeling and it is not to be left behind. Fear will change as will all else. Fear will become the motivator it was meant to be without the pain it now carries. Pain was never meant to be part of fear but they got stuck together and it just happened as many things do. You see, pain belongs in its own place and does not belong attached to fear. Fear is not meant to be a need. It was once a signal also and it has lost its way and been pushed around until it does not know its way.

You will assist pain and you will assist fear. I want you to really begin to concentrate on what frightens you and to know how this fright feels. When you feel fright do you push it away and say, "No, I refuse these feelings." Instead I want you to become part of those feelings and see why they scare you so much. Then I want you to sit in them and absorb them and be part of them and know that they are seeking release and must go somewhere. So, where can they go if you will never allow them to surface? You have been taught from childhood to suppress everything. You have been told to not cry when you wanted to cry and you have been told to not be afraid when you were afraid. No one ever said, "Come on now, we are going to walk you through these feelings and allow them to express themselves."

What if you were beheaded in a past life? Now, in this life, you may see something or even someone who reminds you of that particular trauma. You are now just a child and you have this reminder and so you begin to panic and cry. Your mother and father have no idea what has set you off, and they try to convince you that absolutely nothing is wrong and that you are being silly if you are afraid. So now, you are taught that these feelings have no meaning and that you are simply imagining all of your trauma. Now you are an adult and whenever you get afraid you automatically know that it is just you making something out of nothing. I now want you to realize how there is a reason for everything you experience and express. Begin to see how you are triggered and begin to *allow* the feelings that surface to be. Allow them to express.

Now, when you express, it is not necessary to express to everyone else. Your validity does not lie in everyone else and your "self" does not lie in everyone else. You must learn to associate with you. You must learn to know you as a person and a friend and a lover. You must learn to allow you privacy and even secrecy. You spread things around before you know what they are really about and this causes you further problems. Do not get stuck in certain areas by creating big drama around these areas. I wish to keep you free flowing and unstuck. If you stop to try to teach everyone else you will take much longer to get home. If you stop to explain to everyone else you will more than likely get sidetracked, because others are not you and you are not them. I am not creating separation by this statement. You all know in this course that I speak to you from where you currently stand. We know that we are all one, but we also know that we are individual cells within one being or body. So, as cells, I wish you to focus only on you. You are reading this material because you chose to be at this level at this particular time.

Now, when you begin to express these feelings, that have not been moved in eons, you may have some confusion and discomfort. Feelings are held in mind and the mind is in the cells, which means that "all of you" gets affected since "all of you" is cells. So, if your hair goes limp or your skin gets dry or your breathing gets difficult it is more than likely that a big chunk of stress is exiting. This may occur in cycles and you may get a rest period where you think that it is over and you are back to normal. However, in this school we all know that normal is dysfunctional, and we do not wish to live in what is now the norm, and that is why we are moving "up" to the next level which will not become the norm for some time yet.

So, begin to express this built up charge of fear by taking the time to sit in your fear and feel it, instead of instantly pushing all of those feelings away and trying to feel better. It is sort of like slipping in the mud and falling. Once you get down in it you can roll in it and fling it around and laugh and giggle, or you can simply continue to get upset every time you slip. I think you will enjoy learning about your fear; your feelings... you!

As soon as you begin to discover your true identity you will know that you have a great deal to learn about your own "self." The self is the greatest exploration of all and the self has the greatest depths to be brought up. You will find that most of you know so very little regarding who you are and how you have evolved thus far. You are far greater than you realize and you have never really cared that much about you. You get all involved in discovering inventions and making money but you care little for your own inner workings. You will begin to see how your inner workings have a great deal to do with your outer reality (as you see it). You will find that not only are you complex you are also brilliantly put together. You will begin to see how your layers of belief literally make you up, and how you are or you become what these layers represent. As you begin to discover these various layers you will begin to see how you need not concern yourself with how you are. Someone has already taken a hand in layering you and that same someone must be around yet. Maybe that someone will also assist in taking off those layers.

So, who do we get to assist us in all of this? Who is there that can help? Is it God? Did God assist in the layering and will God assist in the unlayering? Or did God simply allow you to do your own thing while he observed and watched without judgment? Will God always sit back and watch or will God come in now to assist in cleaning up your mess? God does not interfere unless he/she is requested to do so. How can God help if you do not ask? How can God help if you restrict him? God is unlimited and God does not require your help he only requires permission. God will not force you to heal if you like where you are better. God does not force you to be part of him/her if you like being part of something else better.

You are not being part of God by never taking in God. You are part of God by allowing God to be and by allowing God into you. You do not allow by blocking your permission and you do not allow by denial. If you have a big toe but you will not admit that you do, it does not change the fact that you have a big toe. Denial is big enough in you to create any illusion you would like. Do not be so sure that you are not already God. Do not be so sure that God is not already in you and at work in you. Do not be so sure that you are not already moving into God. How would you know? You have so little insight and everything for you is caught up in "outsight." You see nothing that goes on within because you have lost touch with you. You have lost touch with the part of you who is God.

So; as you begin this book I would like you to feel your insides. I want you to begin to literally feel what is moving and taking place inside of you. I want you to feel muscles move and blood pump through your veins and nerve endings sending messages. I want you to feel how active and alive you are. You are a growing, living, pumping plant. You are life, breathing in and out and pulsating. You are a giant cell that is vibrating and a great deal of work is going on inside of you.

So, who runs this work? Who is in charge? Do you think you get kick-started at birth and just keep pumping and vibrating until you die? Or is there something else at work here? Are *you more than* you realize? Are you more complex and powerful than you know? Could it be that you are so advanced that you know how to keep a body going for close to one hundred years without instructions on how to do it? Could it be that you are much more than you ever believed and could it be that you are far greater than anyone has ever suggested? Could it be that you are simply a part of something much greater and that connection to the something greater is what feeds you and keeps you evolving? What could cause such a species to grow and to continue to procreate? Do you think you are like a weed that just accidentally comes up where it is not wanted, or do you think there is a gardener who is tending this vast garden?

Are you in charge of you or are you simply some insignificant part who has little to no say about what is going on? You are no longer going to hide behind the role of the insignificant part. You are going to go into you and realize that you are connected to everything that goes on "in" you; and that connects you to everything that goes on "out" of you. You are going to come out of denial and begin to let go of this little game that you play. You are not a haphazard victim who got caught in something. There is a plan and, believe it or not, you have always known the plan and you okayed it and you created it. So, it is time to begin to reconnect with your own plan and your own self. Get down off your high horse and begin to experience *you* from the inside out. I want you to touch you, to know you, to like you, to really look at you, and best of all I want you to reconnect and want to be you.

You are no longer going to be so confused. When you learn to communicate with your own God you will lose your confusion. You will become one with God and you will become one with your own self. Communication is a two-way street. It is not simply receiving and it is not simply giving. Communication is being one and going in both receiving and giving directions. As you learn to communicate you will be learning about you. You are not only the one who is being discussed you are also the one who is being transformed by discussion. When you begin to ask and receive information regarding your own self you will be literally moving information within yourself. You are made up of vast amounts of information that has been stored in you. To transform or change this information is to transform or change you. You, in communicating with you, will begin to change you. It is all so simple. You become more of you by simply knowing more of you and you become more of you by being more of you.

You are in a position to literally change everything that currently exists regarding who you currently are. You may literally transform to the extent that you will carry all new personality traits and all new insights and even new habits. You may release everything or you may release only a little. For each individual your experience will be different. Allow these differences. I know how you like to accuse others of being weird or off their rocker, but you will learn a great deal if you can learn to allow one another to be completely different without shouting "that's just not possible." Everything is possible and especially now. Now because of the speed and growth taking place and now because you are waking up and seeing more than you have ever seen before.

As you begin to "know thyself," you will begin to "love it or leave it behind." Many habits do not bear any resemblance to what they originally represented. They don't even give you the same satisfaction that you once received. You begin to see how they are not only no longer useful they are totally destructive. So, many habits will go. Habits no longer provide what you desire, as what you desire is return to God and what habits supply is a spinning in one place. As you begin to release old habits and patterns you will be allowing everything to come to you and you will experience from a new perspective. One habit may have been formed in childhood and it may have been used to get you to avoid a situation, or it may have been used to get you to become a part of the situation. There are many aspects of you that are habitual – anything from getting up at a certain time, to sleeping on "your side" of the bed, to calling certain situations dangerous. Sometimes one actually outgrows a fear and yet still gets upset when things occur to remind him or her of the old, now gone, fear.

So, how do we know what is an old fear habit and what is not? We don't need to know. You simply ask to move to awareness and then drop what you no longer wish to carry around and keep what feels good. If it feels good do it. If it doesn't, don't. Pretty simple stuff really. You will often learn that some of what you decide to keep you will later discard also. This is a process of letting go of many parts of you that have kept you grounded, and this letting go will allow you to become lighter and freer. The best way to be light and to be free is to *let go*. "Let go and let God" is still your simplest rule to follow. If you want to get back to God then hand yourself over to God. If you want to be one with God then ask God to take you in and run your life for you.

How often do you ask God to run your life for you? Do you simply ask for that big contract deal to go well or do you say, "God, you do whatever is best in this situation"? Does it scare you to think about letting God run your life? Answer these questions and you will know how much you think of God and God's choices and God's ways. If you do not like God's choices and God's ways you may stay in your own as you have since the beginning of time. If you are truly ready for God, you will allow God to take over for you without fear that God will take away your good. You still have no idea of what good really is. You live in such density that you have never felt good before. You do not yet know the bliss that can be yours once you are unafraid to "let go and let God" take over your life. You think about it for awhile and then you decide.

You will now begin to see how you are part of a giant system that is put together to function. One thing moves another which will engage another which will push at another. What I would like to do is to get you to disengage from this giant system long enough to work on you as a single part. If I can get you to be alone and quiet long enough I can assist you in this healing of the "self." Once the self is healed you will be allowed to reconnect to the entire system and what you have learned will be spread throughout the system. This will assist the entire system and it will allow you space and time to heal on an individual level.

Most of you do not realize the extent of your malfunction or dysfunction. It has become so "normal" to require pills and stimulants that you no longer know how you really feel. Vitamins and other natural ingredients are also put into you on a daily basis to make you feel better or to bring back health. Do you realize that normal is not taking pills or anything to enhance you? Normal is not putting things in to unplug you or to clean out the system. Normal is simply a state of running smoothly off your own juice. So, what happened to you? How did you get so backed up that you began to break down? How did you begin to die? You are dying you know? The system within you is breaking down and falling apart. How will you reverse this process? Well, for one thing you will begin to think positive thoughts, which means that you will begin to know that "absolutely anything is possible." This does not just include what you believe to be outrageously impossible; it also means that whatever crazy things others dream up are possible also. Do not stomp on another's dreams and only hold your own in esteem.

Once you get this very broad and positive attitude you will begin to see how life is all in the making and whatever you wish to make is possible. So, what would you like to make? Is it money? Is it good health? Is it playfulness? Is it joy? Is it peace? What turns you on and lights you up? What do you wish to create first? Well, here is a big hint for you. If you do not deal directly with your dysfunctional attitude and your illness you will not create from love you will create from 'dysfunctionalism' and illness. You will not have a solid ground for your salvation or for whatever choices you believe will bring you the good things that will save you from your current struggle. Salvation comes when you choose and it may start at any area of your life.

Do you wish to save yourself? Then begin to heal yourself. Self-healing will create self-esteem and will elevate you. You will create a good, solid foundation and when you have a good solid foundation you will be able to allow your prosperity in. When you have a shaky or dysfunctioning foundation you cannot possibly create long-term joy or pleasure. Long-term depends on stability not on dysfunction or illness. When you heal you, you will be healing your entire world.

Wellness, as with beauty, is variable for each individual. Some of you who are dying of cancer at this very moment are in better condition spiritually than those who are physically well. Wellness has to do with energy not just the physical body who acts out the beliefs for the soul. The physical body is the next thing to your outer world. It does not manifest into the outer realms until it has a very strong foothold inside. Inside is not simply inside of you physically. Inside is in all of your "field." You are made up of an entire energy field that resonates in or out of balance or harmony. When you are in harmony you create harmony in every area of your life. I will repeat this because it is all you need to know. *When you are in harmony you create harmony.*

It is essential to know that you can create or manifest at any time and you can draw to you what you ask for. Harmony cannot be duplicated by anything but greater harmony. If you wish to create and manifest in your life, I highly suggest that *you* get into balance first. Let everything else be secondary. You will heal you and bring you into balance and then you will automatically draw more of the same. Right now you are out of balance and no matter what you draw or create it will contain this same degree of unbalance. The number one thing to work on is not how to make more money or how to get a bigger house or how to find a perfect relationship. Everything in your life is already in-balance with where you already are (physically, mentally, emotionally, spiritually and many other you's), and how you are. If you continue on this path you will simply create more of the same.

So, why not become solely focused on balancing you. Get you out of dysfunctional behavior and into peace and harmony and the rest of your life will all fall right into place which will be peace and harmony. Do not put all of your energy into building things outside of you when you can use your energy to heal you and everything you want will then simply fall into place. Yes! It is that simple. Things will fall into place and flow for you when you are in-balance and healed. Take the time out of your busy schedule to heal you. I promise you that it will be well worth it. You spend a lot of time searching for instant gratification and when you begin to see how things can actually arrive at your door, without you going out and searching, you will be very surprised and wonder why you spent so many years struggling to get yours, when all you had to do was bring you into balance and your life would flow like crystal clear water flowing into a clear glass.

Do not be so afraid to make working on you a top priority. You create an entire world; actually, you create many worlds. You are well worth taking off some time for. Get it together by getting you together. You are the most valuable thing you have. You desire so much in the way of money and joy and happiness but without "you" all of that has no purpose whatsoever!

We will begin to see just how you are layered and how you are wired to go off. Most of you are so wired and cross wired that you do not realize which direction you should go. You are set up with a list of rules and programs that no longer apply and yet you are hooked up to them. When you begin to see how your wiring is a mess you will begin to rewire your entire system. This will allow you to use your own energy more wisely and it will also allow you to flow within as well as without.

You are now at a point in your evolution that is most important for this very reason. It is a time of change. The old is falling away as the new is being born. Within you, you will begin to see death and birth. Many parts of you will die off and allow new parts to come into awareness. As you see these new parts begin to surface do not be so quick to judge them by your old rules. The old rules will die hard as they have been strongly ingrained in you. You will learn, however, to overcome all previous programming and to move into a future that is free of your old past. In creating this new you, you are literally creating a new future and a new past. As your past changes it assists in the creation of your future. All parts get to move into the light and the past is still alive and part of you.

As you begin to see how you are being moved into your future with a clean slate, you also see how you are being guided through your past in order to release its hold on you. In most cases your past is holding you down and it is in great need of repair. In most cases your past is no longer part of you in that you have buried it or pushed it out of you. The past must be reclaimed in order to rise up to the next level. You bring all of you with you. When you are climbing up onto a new plateau you do not get your head and arms to the top of it and say, "Okay, I am here, I have arrived." You pull *all* of you up onto the level surface and then you stand up and shout, "Yes! I made it, I'm all here."

So, as you rise to each new level you take all of you, and you do not leave your legs or your back end hanging off the edge wondering what to do. Be kind to all of you. You have created many you's and they are all floating around you and attached to you. It does not matter how strongly you wish to forget them, they are still there and ignoring them does about as much good as ignoring dirt and dust that is building up on your desk at home. At some point your workplace is going to become too cluttered and too dusty to work from. At that time you will be smart to begin to clean house to know where everything is so that you might have an efficient work center. If you never clean off your desk you may die under the clutter of dirt and debris. The least that will happen is that you will no longer have a smooth working situation. The worst that will happen is that the clutter will take over you.

As you begin to see how you are no longer being stuck in your past and you begin to unstick it by seeing it as a cycle or pattern, you will be able to rise above that particular cycle. You will become "aware" of the pattern. If you have a habit of knocking your pencil on your desk while someone is speaking to you it may become quite annoying to others and they may not wish to speak with you. So, you learn to spot these tendencies and then, when you begin to knock your pencil, you might remind yourself, "Oh, this is not such a good idea. It drives people crazy and no one will want to speak with me." Now you have begun to change your old pattern or cycle. In past lives the patterns are a little bigger and stronger. In past lives you have a habit of raping and pillaging and plundering and you have certain people in your life who were with you or against you in those lives. When you reconnect with these people you will fall back into your same patterns quite easily. You will want to hurt those who have hurt you. You will want to make amends to those you unjustly harmed and you will want to love those who loved you.

Now, the trick is that these feelings are based on past lives. Often in past lives you are dealing with your other past lives as well. So, as you begin to get to know someone you begin to remember through psychic awareness that they once did this or that to you. Now your mental awareness picks up your psychic memories and it begins to go "on guard." You begin to mistrust this person and you begin to mistrust your own mistrust of this person. You are confused by your own signals because this person has not done anything to you (in this life).

So, how can we let go of this type of judgment and allow freedom from the past? I would say that your best bet is to "trust God." Allow God to walk in your shoes for you because God is not caught up in the psychic drama nor the karmic drama. God will simply walk you through each situation and not act out, or react, to the new situation from a level of "charge" that is obviously attached to the old situation. Just "stay calm and breathe peace" and allow God to carry you through. Any created situation is going to reflect the issues of the past. If you have strong issues with a person it will be acted out strongly again. That is unless you stop! If you can "not react so strongly" and "not respond so actively" you will take the charge off of your entire cycle of karma with this particular individual.

If they killed you in a past life, your hatred could draw them to you in this life and you have probably killed them many times before also. You now "attract" one another because you are connected by this charge. Love/hate is very strong and has a big charge. Often a parent is raising someone they have killed in order to balance that aspect. Often a child is being rebellious because the child remembers and wants no part of the parent. This all gets very crossed and mixed and your wiring is totally out of control in this area. It's a game you play called incarnate and die. It's a game that got all messed up and now you are straightening it out and cleaning up your mess. You are clearing the air so to speak. You are getting this nonsense out of the way so that you might have peace instead of war. You are tired of the war game and you want to create peace, and to do so you must discharge a few old explosives that are lying around and you must clean up the mess that has served as your playground.

You are cleaning out old parts of you in order to change your habit from "irritating one another into anger" to "loving one another into peace." It will work. You will get through this mess and you will see everything differently. You will no longer go off the deep end simply because someone said this or that to push your buttons. You will become balanced by discharging the old debts you believe you owe to one another. The game is over. Karma is no longer an option. No one is going to go for "an eye for an eye" anymore. It's going to be smooth sailing from now on. You are going to stop intentionally irritating one another.

You will begin to realize just how close to God you have come when you begin to see peace and calm enter your life. When you begin to experience a new calmness and peacefulness you can imagine how good you will feel. You will have left your big traumas behind you and you will have come fully into you. You are simply a cell that is coming into consciousness after being totally unconscious. You are God and have always been; only now you will have the awareness of the connection that is God. You will begin to know the truth and to be who you wish to be instead of who you were trained to be. A mad dog is not always a good guard dog and you need no longer pretend to be a guard dog and defend yourself. You will find that as you let go of more and more of your programming and training, you will be able to stand in front of others and not be afraid. You will not fear their criticism and you will not yearn for their acceptance. You will simply be happy to be you.

When you get to this level you will be very well received because you will no longer have any issues around being received. Once you begin to see how you create and draw to you all that you are, you will begin to see how you can let go of some of what you are. Many of you will realize that you actually are what you do not wish to be and this has caused problems and a big battle within you. You have had traits and behavioral patterns that are inherited and passed from parent to child and again from that child to his/her children. For the sake of your own health and welfare you are now releasing these unnecessary and outdated rules, habits, phobias, beliefs, ideas and judgments. You are going to be you without all the clutter and debris that has always cast a shadow over you. You are going to become all that you are by letting go of all that you have become. Most of what you have become is based on earth teachings and earth wisdom and earth knowledge. This worked for a time but it is now outdated and unnecessary.

You are moving into a new era, and this new era will become all that you wish as long as you let go of all of your past programming which only wishes to protect, defend and be right. There was a great glory in being right when it was important. It is no longer important. It is not necessary and it is not even welcome in most cases. Your "need to be right" can actually cause heated arguments and hurt feelings. And what does it really matter who is right and who is not? It is not important in a world where there is no wrong. In a world where everyone is simply left alone to create you will not find such silliness. In a world where creation is simply taking place for the pure pleasure of it you will never have need or use for right and wrong. In a world where everything is done out of pleasure and joy there is no desire to say that your creation is better than mine or my creation is greater than yours. You will not need to be over achievers or under achievers. You will simply do what feels good.

Did you ever sit and watch nature? The birds and butterflies and bears and cats and dogs and turtles and fish do what feels good to them. No rules of right or wrong. They flow with creation. They play and nap and have a very nice time. Leave creation alone and you will be leaving you alone. You are acting like a trained bear in a circus. You act a certain way because you were born into it and "trained." Now is the time to discover who you really are and have been all along. If you release a bear who has always been in captivity he will be very confused about nature and his reality. He only knows what he knows. What he knows is learned; taught. What he knows is trained behavior. Put him in the wild with others who are wild and he will adapt in time. You do not simply give up on him and put him in a cage in old age when he can no longer perform for you. Or do you? Is this how you were trained to do things? You only know what you know, and what you know is trained behavior. I am now telling you that you can un-train you by learning how you were trained and seeing it through adult eyes and letting it go.

In the letting go lies your freedom. As you view your patterns of behavior you will find that you will not readily give up a pattern. You want to hold on to what feels "right" for you because it makes you "right." When you learn to let go of right and allow yourself to be wrong you will no longer feel the need for punishing you every time you do something the old you believes to be wrong. You see, punishment goes hand-in-hand with being wrong. If you get wrong answers in school you get bad grades. Bad grades mean a stupid or problem child. Problem children are undesirable and not a good thing. Poor grades from wrong answers also lead to direct punishment. Some of you were hit, some were spoken to harshly and some got the silent treatment. Others lost going out privileges or television privileges. Either way you were taught to give the right answer and now you often fake it when you are not sure what the right answer is.

Some of you are so afraid of not giving the right answer that you get upset at the person asking the question. You want to be right but how can you if you don't know how to answer from truth, as you know that the truth will not be acceptable? How do you deal with giving the right answer when you are being questioned by another who is *trained* to be right? You each come from different truths and you each expect a right answer. Stop expecting right answers and you will begin to flow. You will be allowed to move on if you do not get so hung up on the answers you get. When someone has a need to be right allow it. It has no basis in spirituality because it does not exist anywhere but on earth. There is really no such thing as right or wrong so stop fighting over it.

We will learn that there is no such thing as not wanting to be God. To say that you do not want to be God is like a flower saying "I do not want to bloom." No one is more important to you than God. God is the part of you who allows you to continue. God is the source of all that you are and God is the source of all that is. To say you do not need God is like a human saying I do not need a heart. God is your heart and God is your center. You sprouted from God and you cannot be anything but God. God is what you are and God is how you are. You will find that you no longer require your God to hide. You will find that God will begin to move to the forefront and God will begin to take over for you. You will begin gradually so as not to frighten yourself. Everything seems to frighten you and so you will be afraid as God begins to emerge.

Remember the analogy I gave you about giving birth to God? Well, if you were giving birth for the very first time and no one, or very few, had ever given birth before you would not know what was happening. Think of when the baby's head begins to emerge from the womb. Who would explain for you that this big round thing between your legs is a good thing? You would be terrified until you saw that it was actually a head attached to a body. At that point you would either pass out in shock or be totally mystified at such a miracle.

Babies being born are much like God being born. God is coming into this dimension and you are providing the vehicle. With a baby, you provide the vehicle for another soul to enter. So; why doesn't God just appear or burst out of the sky in glorious living color? You are God! You are all part of God and God is simply showing you who you are and have always been. God is no longer going to be seen as a separate entity who does not touch you and who you do not touch. You do touch God. You are God. You are a living cell that is God consciousness, and that cell is so important to the whole that it is the totality of the whole. Every cell reflects the universe and every universe reflects the totality of creation.

When you first begin to "feel" God, you will feel a little uncomfortable. You have never felt this part of yourself before and this is the part that you so desperately tried to shut down. This is the part that does not judge. This is the part who is kind and loving and graceful. You will learn that although you are all God you have shut down certain parts of you. Some of you shut down your anger so you would not have to deal with your own violent nature. With your anger went your pleasure. When you shut down your displeasure you also shut off your pleasure. So, if you are one of those who tried to control your violence by shutting down your anger you probably have very little pleasure in your life.

Turn you back on! It is all God and it serves a purpose. You have distorted the use of your emotional body to the extent that it is all tied in knots. Do you feel tense and a little stressed at times? You should see what your emotional body looks like. Let me explain it this way. If you had a road map in front of you with all the primary highways marked in one color (say red), and all the through roads marked in another color (say black), and all of the intermediary roads marked in a color (say yellow), and maybe some new routes of travel in another color (blue), you would then pick up this imaginary map and turn it upside down. As you do so the roads, highways, freeways and streets literally fall off the map. You now have a jumble of string like (webbing) material that is all piled up, and when you try to pick it up it will often break because it is so fine and sheer.

As you pick it up it also becomes more tangled. Now you have a big glob of matted-up blue and black and yellow and red. You have a mess that was once a smooth running plan to guide you to your destination. So many of your roads got blocked and thrown off the map that there is no map left. So many fine lines have been pushed to their breaking limit and you are now the result. We have walking, talking, nervous breakdowns and it is all due to emotional shut down. When you shut down your emotions you create huge emotional jumbles inside of you, and these emotional blocks are preventing you from rising to your full potential which is God. Now we are going to straighten this mess out and create a new road map that really flows.

Do not shut down your emotions and do not be afraid of your emotions. Get them "up" and unblocked. Use your emotions. You were always taught not to yell and scream so you trained yourself to stop. Now when your emotions are screaming you are holding it in and killing the body in the process. When your emotional body needs to relieve itself it is no different than when the physical body needs to relieve itself. You have never been taught to love and nurture your physical body so how do you expect to know how to love and nurture your emotional body? This body is very fragile and has a great deal of healing to do.

I expect you to know already how to release your emotionally pent-up charge. You get a pillow and beat up your bed or you drive your car out of town and scream at the top of your lungs. You have all read this in our last book and I do not expect you to be reading this information if you have not yet read Book Fourteen, *Illumination*. You are very fragile and you must begin to nurture and care for all parts of you. You need not shock your system by reading what you are not equipped to handle and you need not push yourself any further than you are willing to go.

So, for now I want you to unblock your anger and let it out. This does not mean that you go out and tell people off, it does not mean that you give anyone a piece of your mind (you need all you've got), and it does not mean that you yell at the kids or your spouse or that you kick your dog. You simply release anger constructively and you create a safe space to do so, also a private space. No big drama please. You are the only one who is necessary to heal you.

⁂

You will be the most happy when you have let go of your struggle to maintain your rules. You have rules that apply to you because you were taught to use rules. It is most difficult for you to let go of them because you believe they are right. You do not wish to be wrong and to make a mess of things so you continue to believe that you are right and therefore in the good. Anyone who is wrong is automatically in the bad and so you now have categorized your world into good guys and bad guys.

No one is good or bad. Everyone is God. How can you make that analogy fit into your narrow world of good vs. bad? You cannot. You would have to make some parts of God bad and some parts good. You would have to divide God and separate God. This is what you have done. You created your own version of God and you said, "Okay, this is evil and does not exist for God or in God." And then you took other parts and you said, "Okay, this is good and deserves to be part of God." Then you took what you liked and taught it and you threw out the rest. You deny God because you do not know what to do with all of God. You deny God because you do not have the ability to see beyond your nose. Your limited point of view has given you a limited view of God.

Now God is going to become "all that is" and this type of separation is going to end. God is whole, and you are no longer going to look upon God and judge what is acceptable and what is not. All is part of God. All is God and God is all. Nothing is left out of God. Just because you have been *taught* to hate certain traits does not make these traits not God. You must learn to accept and allow all parts of God to be. You are not happy with God and so you chop God up into neat little pieces and you say, "Okay, this is good and this is a no-no." You cannot continue in this fashion. You are so confused that you are mislabeling and messing up your own creation. When you begin to see "all" for what it really is you will see what a big mistake you have made in calling things bad or evil. You will want to change this when you become aware of how *you* are creating bad or evil simply by your belief in it. You will wish to change how you dissect God and get rid of parts you have no understanding for. When you learn to understand and when you learn to use your awareness, you will find that you will have use for all parts and you will wish to keep all parts.

As you begin to discover how you belong to all parts and all parts belong to you, you will see how those parts that you hate and try to cut out of God are the parts that you have tried to cut out of you. As you discover what these parts are you may begin to integrate them back into the whole. You may put God back together by allowing everything to be in perfect and divine order. This allows all parts to "be." And it also allows all parts to know that they "are" and that they are no longer being pushed away from God. As parts return, they become what they have always been which is God force. God force is perfect and divine and has a purpose. You may not see God's purpose but then you are not fully grown nor are you developed. You are at an elementary stage in your evolution and you do not see what is here. You are partially blind and partially stunted in your education. You took a giant step into ignorance and darkness and now you are moving into enlightenment and "light."

You will find that the majority of you have very little information on God. You only know what you have learned from the past, and the past was even more fearful than the present. You are actually moving out of the darkness so why would you bring forward the teachings that kept you in darkness? Why not let go of the dark past with all its superstition and move into the future with an open and empty mind? Yes, that's it, *empty your mind.* Stop repeating old programs and buying into old beliefs. Be a whole new you. Be a blank memory bank that is ready to learn the truth. Don't bring any baggage with you. Everything that you need will be supplied.

As you move into this bright new future you will learn that your old ways and old teachings have no usefulness. They were designed to get you where you are now and we are moving you from now into when. As you move from now to when, you will want to let go of then. Then was then. Now is now and when will be when. Do not be afraid of when. If you live totally in the now you will automatically move into when. Now is geared to get you to when, but most of you are still in back then.

As you learn to disconnect and let go you will learn to *move without fear.* Moving without fear is a very good thing. Moving without fear is trusting where you are, and trusting where you are will get you where you want to be. You want to be in joy, peace and happiness. I know you still request money, a good job, health and someone to love but what you are searching for is *joy*, *peace* and *happiness.* Asking for specifics gets you into your own tangled web of conditioning and programming. I highly suggest that you focus on what you really want which is joy, peace and happiness. Ask for these daily and look for them in every situation until you begin to find them. When you do please say, "thank you" and continue to ask and receive more of the same.

You will now find that you are in a most unusual position. You are in touch with all that you judge and so you begin to "feel" your judgment. When you first begin to discover all that you have pushed down and denied, you will begin to know that you are no longer in a position to hide parts of you. These parts are coming to the surface and they are going to be felt and experienced on some level. If you begin to get a little irritable or out of sorts just remember that you are facing all your "wrongs" and "bads." Anything that you thought was bad or wrong will present itself to you so that you may decide to call it "okay" and allow it to simply "be."

All parts of you will be presented to you for your approval. You may change what you do not like but it is best to at least allow it to be. You need never judge parts of you as bad or wrong. Simply allow all parts to be and see how you might find use for them. You are not here to find fault with God. You are here to accept God and to allow God to be part of you. You are not allowing your own essence and your own source to be you. You are blocking and creating dark holes where energy once moved freely. Do not create dark holes. Be as kind as you can be to all parts of you. Love you and nurture you for you are God. If you can learn to love you and nurture you, you will be loving and nurturing God.

As you begin to see how you have pushed parts of you down into these dark holes, you will begin to see how darkness is not separate from light. They are one and the same energy. They belong together and work together. After all, it would be very difficult to see the beauty of a bright star without the night to illuminate it. How would you see a big, round, white moon without the dark sky that surrounds it? A flame burns beautifully in a silent, dark room. Darkness creates contrast for light and it is now time to accept what we believe to be dark. After all, we could not see a movie from a projector without the darkness in the room. We cannot see a great deal without contrast created by darkness.

As you begin to learn more and more about yourself, you will begin to see how you will no longer be hiding. You are coming out of the darkness to see who you are. Do not be afraid of who you are. Do not deny you and do not criticize you. It is only your training that has ever taught you evil. You would not believe in bad if you were not taught that "No, this is wrong" and "Yes, that is the right way." Make up your own way now. Find a new path to walk and call everything good. Find a purpose for everything that you hate or despise or loath. There is a gift in everything! Absolutely everything has a useful purpose. Everything is God! God *is* everything! How can anything possibly be evil or awful? It is not.

You have a great deal to learn and it is a gradual process. The transformation from dark to light is simply the switching on of you. You are going to turn on and light up all of you. You are going to accept and embrace all parts of you. You are going to love and accept you totally. This will be the very first time you have been allowed to see this far into you. You have never before walked this particular path into you. You have tried many forms of release and have not ever decided to simply go within and look at who you are. God has always been perceived as outside of you and that is where you search for God and for love. Now you are going to find how love is in you and you are in love. When you find the love in you, you will be in direct contact with God. God is love and love is God. God is everywhere and love is everywhere.

As you begin to discover how you do not wish to be in the dark any longer, you will come forward into the light of awareness and you will allow the dark to continue to do its job. The dark is representative of many things, and its primary job or function is to create space in which the light might do its job. One embraces the other, and to cut off one is to lose the other also. You do not shut down darkness and still return to the light. You do not embrace the light without receiving the dark and embracing the dark. Everything has a plus and a minus and everything has two sides. Once you get both sides into balance you may sit somewhere in the middle and enjoy the best of both worlds. If you push at darkness you stretch the distance between your polarities and it becomes a greater extreme.

In most cases light and dark have been pushed very far away from each other and the space between is filled with controversy. You have stretched things as far as they are willing to go at this time, and it is now time to allow this space to close and bring these two polarities together. Light and dark belong together. Just as you have a right and a left for balance so does creation have a right and a left. If you take away your left leg you do not stand so well on just your right. All of creation is meant to be in perfect balance with a right and a left. You need not agree, but it is true. You need only know that it is time to bring your left into balance with your right.

You are well beyond the turning point now. You have come this far and you have seen how you create your own reality and how you are your reality. You may change what you see by changing you. You are the one who is in charge and you are the one who creates and imagines and dreams and holds on to belief. If you can learn to work with you and within your own limited view you can actually expand that view. You may be able to take on a much broader perspective by rising "up" to a new level and allowing all that you view to be acceptable. You do not have to direct and produce and choreograph every move that creation makes. Allow God and creation to be. Leave God alone. Stop trying to put God into a neat organized slot so that you can feel safe. Allow God to be everything – even the things you personally do not approve of. Stop separating God into good and bad or can and can't. *God is!* He/she is not for you to create. He/she already is and has always been. God is. God is. God is.

You will not find anywhere in God a place that is not God. You will not find anywhere in creation a thing that did not come from God. You will not find anywhere in thought a thought that did not come from God. So, if God is all and all is God, you are God and the one you hate is God. How many do you hate? How many do you believe to be beneath you? You are putting parts of you "down." You are creating places that do not exist and you are cubby-holing parts of you because you are afraid of them. How did you get afraid of you? How did you begin to fear your own feelings and your own thoughts? You began by saying that something was wrong or bad. Now, every time a feeling comes to the surface you try to shut it off because you are afraid of your own feelings. Fear is such a feeling. Nervousness is another. You are all so afraid of the feeling of being nervous that you avoid situations that might make you nervous. Nervousness is not acceptable to you because you are not in control.

When you find yourself in your fear and out of control, or not in control, I wish you to remember that this is a body signal that is meant to work with you and not against you. Begin to accept and to embrace all bodily functions so that you do not shut down any more of your physical self than necessary. When you are nervous or upset I want you to "feel" it. I want you to really get into it and not try to push it away. As a matter of fact you can bring on more of the same and really learn to embrace it. What is it that upsets you so much that you instantly want these feelings to go away? What is your fear or mistrust of these feelings attached to? How can you be so upset when nothing is really going on? You know that everything is illusion and everything is okay so let your feelings in on this. Do not block your feelings and do not push them away. Begin to allow them their space and they will not have the power or charge behind them that they now carry.

You were once so dependent on feelings that you did not require logic. Now you have switched over into logic and you do not trust, nor do you use your feelings. This is shutting down a very big and powerful part of you. This is why so many are out of control and going to doctors for nervous breakdowns. No one can handle their own feelings. The problem is not what others might do or say to you. The problem is how you "feel" and respond to what others do and say. Others are not the problem. Your inability to handle your own feelings is the problem. So, now that you know I wish you to begin to get in touch with how you feel. Acknowledge your rage and your fear. Acknowledge your confusion and your pain. This is not to be done with another. You need not run to your neighbor and say, "Wow, I just found out I have rage and am very afraid of my own rage." He would use this to his advantage simply because he too has confusion and rage. Do not turn you over to another. Begin to see how you like to get approval and show off for another's attention.

You all seek attention in your own personal way. This is not about getting attention or energy to support you from outside of you. This is about getting "free to be you." You get free to be you by knowing you and accepting all parts of you, not by getting your neighbor or lover or best friend or even your mother to accept you. Allow you to stand alone because, in this, you are alone. No one is inside of you but you. You are the one who is healing and becoming whole. You do not become whole by continually looking outside of you for support and approval. Look to you. You are your own source of light. You are connected to God. You are not connected to your neighbor who is connected to God. You are your own connection and your neighbor is his own.

You will begin to see how no one is you and you are no one else. You are simply you and you need not tell another how to get from point A to point B. No one is in you so no one knows how you are mapped out. You also do not know how anyone else is mapped out. Most of you spend a great deal of time telling those you claim to love how to live and how to be. Do you wonder why you do not tell outsiders what to do so much as you do your own spouse or children? It is because you believe that you own them. You believe you have a right to dictate how they should or should not do things. This, of course, is all caught up in the fact that you spend your money on them and you believe they owe you something in return. You like to call the shots and you like to be left alone as sole ruler. If you can just learn to allow yourself to be, you will automatically begin to give up your need to rule over and lord over others.

You all have this need. It is like a pecking order of sorts. Big brother gets to lord over and be in charge of the younger siblings, and parents are calling the shots over all. Sometimes one parent is dominant and the other is being lorded over also. This is usually the case. Then you have law and order which reigns outside the home and a government that lords over its citizens. When you bring it back down to the sibling level, the smallest child will have a toy or doll or cat to take it all out on. It has to go somewhere. The chain of command does not simply end. It goes until it no longer exists, which is when there is no bug or rock or stick to take things out on.

You are now beginning to break free of this type of behavior. You will begin to see how a pecking order only creates situations that are undesirable. At this time you are teaching yourself to keep what is desirable and healthy and let go of whatever might clog up your flow to the top. You will find that authoritarian ways clog the wheels of success from turning. You get stuck in all the should's and shouldn'ts, and you do not know how to move forward.

Once you begin to look at who you are, you will see how you have been programmed by authority and you must now break out of that mold that you are still in. Do not be an authority, it will slow you down. Do not be "sure" and "certain" and "right" about everything for it will clog your system and it will cause you to get stuck in your certainty, and you will be so sure of who you are and what you think you are that you will not want to move "up" into Godness, which is flexible and moving and uncertain and unsure. How can you accept God if you are so busy standing your ground and being right? Allow yourself to be insecure and to tiptoe around the issues without getting stuck to them or in them. Do not be afraid to not be an authority. I know this will be difficult, as you have been programmed by other authoritarians and you are what you were programmed to be.

"Let go!" Let everything go and simply jump into the chasm that is being presented. It is a void and it will give you the space to not ground yourself and to float free of restrictions. A chasm need not be a bottomless pit of doom. It may be a space in which to float free and not be on the ground or in the clouds. It may be a hole that does not go down but allows you the time to buffer your actions with non-action. If you fall into a chasm you will still be in the earth but not on it. You will be a step closer to moving "up" by your ability to let go. Let go! Be unafraid, and do not require that you follow the rules laid down by the authoritarians who came before you. You are never right because there is nothing to be right about. The minute you decide it is night and dark it will all change and become day and light.

You cannot win by being right. Right is a controversy in terms. Nothing is one way or another. All of creation is both ways. You have created polarity where it does not exist. Once you learn how to avoid changing things you do not understand, you will become better at simply allowing everything to flow. There is form to everything. There is a flow. There is a pattern. There is beauty. There is grace. You will learn that, within the flow, you will find the surrender that is required for you to give up your harsh ways and allow for softer living. You will flow by being subtle not by being rigid. Let go of your need to be a "know it all" and you will be letting go of a very heavy part of you.

You are now in a position to become whole. You are moving toward your center and allowing the duality of your existence to merge. As you allow duality to merge, you will begin to see how no one is left out of this entire process. This entire process is like putting together two sides of the page and folding it in half to show that it is still intact and yet smaller. It is the same page with all the same words or information on it, but it is now half the size. Then when you fold it again it will be even smaller. Nothing is missing from it but it is folding in on itself and becoming less. In this way it can easily be stored in an envelope and removed by whoever wishes to read the information on the page. Nothing changes except the page gets smaller and takes up less space. Is the page really smaller or is it simply taking up different space? Now instead of being paper thin and measuring a specific size it is smaller in size and thicker. The thickness has expanded as the length and width contracted. It was once spread out and now it is confined. It is the same letter or words or information on the same piece of paper but now the page is in a different shape.

You are being reshaped! You are bringing all parts of you in on you in order to know you. As you experience all parts of you, you will have the opportunity to know and embrace the four corners of your duality. You will be allowed to experience yourself folding in on you to make you less spread out and more easily slipped through the envelope of time/space and into the world of truth. As you begin this process you will be allowed to take yourself into various levels of creation without consciously going anywhere. You will be able to slip through space and time by your ability to fold yourself into yourself. You will be able to pass through time shifts that will allow you to perceive time from a whole new perspective. You will be allowed to cross dimensions and you may not even realize that you have done so.

You may begin to shift up to a new level, and it will take a little time before you begin to realize how things have changed for you. You will be moving so quickly that you will feel only a little different and maybe have a "sense" that you are about to create something new, or that something new has just been created. Either way you will be experiencing from a position of bringing *your* time/space into a smaller portion of the universe. Time/space is very subjective and so are you. You will find that as you begin this process of folding in on yourself, you will be required to bring the two sides of you together. East and West will meet. Right and wrong will be layered over one another.

Out of this will come great change, great controversy and great upset. Out of the change and controversy and upset will come a new world order. You will have successfully healed the split between God and man. You will be in a position to reach out and touch God! God will be on top of man instead of out there somewhere. Talk about things falling on you to get your attention! God is going to be folded over onto man and God and man will merge into one to take a new shape just as your page has done. This is what is occurring now for many of you. You are being guided in many ways to become all that God is, and to become all that God is you must become all that you are.

You are God and you are also man. You will merge and become "one" and you will know that God is actually all things and you are actually all things. This is still in the works and you will be seeing its results soon. All is taking place for each individual at their own speed. Everyone gets to wake up and know God. Some run the race sooner than others. It has already been done as everything has. It is only a matter of when each individual will choose to run this particular movie on their own inner screen. We all get to select our own movies depending on what we are ready for. I just thought you might like to know that this particular movie is now available for those who wish to view it.

You will begin to discover how you have always been afraid. You will begin to see your fears and experience those you wish to release. On a larger level you are fearless and you do not wish to carry this seed of fear. As you begin to release your fears you may become anxious and panic easily. This is natural. It is not a long term situation and you will learn to release by feeling your emotions rather than pushing them away. As you learn to feel your emotions you will begin to experience the fact that you are living inside of you. Things need not change for you to change. Often, simply receiving information can have a huge effect on you. Nothing need occur directly to you to set you off. Sometimes you are so attached to the lives of others that what occurs in their lives becomes a stimulant, or depressant, in yours. You allow yourself to get all caught up in emotional turmoil because you are so in need of stimulation. Some of you can watch the news and get all riled up. It's best to cease this type of stimulation until you have moved into some degree of balance.

For the most part you are a giant jumble of miswiring and it is best to keep your stimulation at a minimum until you can learn to know peace; calm; tranquility. You will find your life boring and you wish to stir things up again but try to enjoy the boredom when it arrives. Do not push it away in favor of excitement and action. Most of the action you create is so dramatic that it takes you months to settle back down and get calm. No more drama in your life is needed. Keep it plain and simple. You will find that everything will flow when you are flowing; no big ups and downs, no big trauma and no big pain.

You will find that you are new to this game of floating. You only know how to go way up and way down. It seems to be your pattern. You seem to get upset or excited and then you get bored and depressed. Learn to float through such emotions and stay somewhere in the middle. Do not exit and try to escape your feelings by going out of body. The first signs of this are depression and over excitement. When your emotions get out of control you usually try to control them or stuff them down so you will not have to deal with them. Use this opportunity to deal with them. This is part of you that you are denying by pushing it away. Accept all parts of you and learn to know all parts of you. You will be happy you did.

When you begin to evolve to a level where you no longer create the ups and downs you will begin to flat line. This is a term used to show death on a monitor and this is what will be reflected by you as you reach this stage. You will be balanced. You will not be exciting and/or depressing. You will be flat. You will have personality, but your emotional charge will be discharged to the extent that you are floating in one place instead of bouncing all over the place. You may not like this at first. You are so accustomed to stimulation and to bouncing all over the place that to be "calm" is going to be a let down from your highs. It will also be a "lift" from your lows. When you can learn to float and not stir things up, you will be able to float in the source without stirring up everything that is in the source. The source is the ultimate creation and the source contains anything that can be thought. To bounce around in the source is to stir up a lot of creative and destructive power. Remember, everything has its opposite, and when you are bouncing around out of control you hit a great deal of potential for both creativeness and for destructiveness.

Now; when you float in the source you can be directed by the source itself. It is like a stream with a current. When you are bouncing all over the place you create from all directions. When you are floating in the source, the source will carry you in its direction or current. You can be a fish swimming upstream and struggling to get there or you can stay calm and "float" in this current of the source. The current will take you gradually and gently where you need to go. The current flows through every part of the source without disturbing the source. You have this giant pool of creative power and it's time to stop jumping in and doing belly flops. Just slip in and float. Let the current take you where the current is going. What have you got to lose?

You will begin to see how you are not only made up of emotional charge, you are also made up of judgments that create beliefs and certain responses to those beliefs; and it is best now to let go of all judgment and allow your beliefs to flow. The more you can allow your beliefs to flow the more you will flow. You are made up in vast part by your beliefs and to know something for certain will stick you in certainty. Begin to see how beneficial it might be for you to not be stuck. Begin to see how you might let go of your hold on a right-way/wrong-way mentality. You are being unhooked and untrained. The fastest way to untrain you is to wipe out all of your programming and allow you to start over with a clean slate. You will find that you no longer require justice or karma once you give up right and wrong.

You will begin to see that you are never in your right place which is also a fixed position. To say you have a right place implies very strongly that you have a wrong place. All through this series I have spoken to you from where you are and from within your own vocabulary with your words and your sense of what is real. As I begin to move you out of your reality and into freedom, you may find duality or conflict in statements. This is due to the fact that *everything is,* and you have a tendency to allow only partial reality. You do not even allow for fifty percent to come through. You cut off everything that you do not understand and what you are left with is very small indeed. Most of you are bored with life because you allow so little life or creation in. Everything is possible and yet you only will allow one way to exist, and then you cut reality down further by placing restrictions on your one way. You have a myriad of choices but you allow so few through.

As you begin to see how this affects you and changes reality, you will want to open to a broader sense of who you are and allow more of you in. This is also part of what you are learning to develop. You are learning to let all of you out. You are learning to allow you to "be" without pushing you back down into the subconsciousness or into the darkness. As you learn to allow more of you to come through, you will begin to see a change in how you perceive others. You will begin to see how no one is actually a villain and, on the other hand, how no one is actually a victim. These will be the first big façades to go.

No more believing in a victim so you will have no one to defend. If you have no one to defend, you will have no reason to attack. If you do not attack what will you do?

You will become peaceful beings. You will begin to see how life is not just what you thought it was. Life is everything whether you want to accept it or deny it. The benefit in accepting is that you then get to share in it. You can only walk in what you create or allow to be created. If you do not allow it you are cut off from it. You will find that you do not wish to be left out of God and all that is God. As you begin to accept this part of you, you will begin to see extraordinary results. The results of allowing God to be in charge are quite powerful and will be felt on many levels. Your changes and shifts in consciousness may be subtle but you will be moving in a big way. All of you will be involved meaning "all parts of you." You will not leave any part of you out of God. All parts are you and, therefore, all parts are affected by this change or shift.

Now; when you begin to realize that you are changing, you will not always know how to act or respond to life. You may begin to walk with a certain amount of confusion and even over-sensitivity. You may begin to bring up so much fear that your daily life becomes one big release of fear. You may begin to trigger very large amounts of old "charge" to the surface. This will be felt as nervousness and over-excitement. In many cases the old "charge" coming to the surface will be lethargic. This is due to the fact that you have literally been paralyzed in your fears at certain points in your evolution. This will often surface as dysfunctional behavior toward others and a sense of being stuck with no way out.

As you begin to clear all "charges" that have been stuck in you since the beginning of time, you will want to know that you need not repeat every situation you have ever created in any life you have lived. It is only necessary to clear the immediate problem that is holding you back. Usually this problem will be repeated through several past lives and will be the same problem you have been working on and never solved. The reason you cannot solve a problem karmically is that you cannot do-to-yourself one lifetime in order to repent for what you did-to-them in the past. You are using "an eye for an eye" mentality and it does not work, it only creates a cycle.

Now; when you can let go of karma and let go of the belief that you need to do it until you get it right, you will learn that it does not matter what you do. You do not have to come back and punish yourself to get even. Some of you come back to punish others to get even. *Let it all go!* Stop this karmic nonsense. You do not need to justify yourself to God... not ever.

So; I want you to stop believing that if you are bad you will come back and pay for it. Stop believing that if you do not learn you will come back to learn. Stop sticking yourself in these non-productive, go-nowhere beliefs. You sit and spin your wheels. You need not come back for any reason and you do no wrong!

You will begin to see how you are no longer stuck in the universal flow when you begin to move out of your normally logical behavior. You will begin to know that you do not belong stuck when you begin to feel the need for change. When you feel the need for change it is part of your own growth. Often you simply do not require the same old ways and are seeking new ways. When you begin to look for new ways you will find your own in-depth ability to create from the flow.

The flow is always available and it is never ending. You may choose to remain in any part of the flow of life. If you wish to remain in a tiny stream you will get smaller doses of creation. If you move into the mainstream you get much larger doses of creation. When you are in the flow it is very difficult for you to know where the flow is taking you. You have all been taught to get a grip on your life and have control over your life. No one has ever taught you to let go and ride the flow. You do not know how to flow simply because you have been taught to do the opposite. You will find that as you learn to let go of control you will be allowing creation to enter you. You will be allowing the creative force to enter simply by nonresistance.

You are by now moving into new levels of consciousness. This has been created simply by drawing your thoughts into new areas of you. This is done easily enough. Printed words have the ability to produce a direction for the reader to follow. In this way you are guided into areas of you that you would not know exist. When you begin to see how your consciousness is shifting you will begin to realize that change is inevitable and already in the works. As you begin to feel change you will begin to sense a loss. All change brings birth of new and shedding of old. So, as you feel this loss you may get upset and you may get angry. It is a necessary loss. It is part of the shift, and you will not see it as a loss once you have arrived at a new level of awareness. Then you will look back and see it as change and growth. Some of you do that now with past experiences. Maybe you had a lover who left you only to be replaced by someone new. Or maybe you had a friend who moved away only to be replaced by a new friend.

In the case of your consciousness, new thoughts are constantly replacing old thoughts and old thoughts are constantly going. So, where do these old thoughts go and how do you get new thoughts? It is all in the source. The universal thought pool has it all. You can try on one thing and if it does not feel good you put it back and try on something else. It is like trying on clothes. Some things feel better to you than they do to your neighbor and vice versa. When you begin to understand the style that you feel best in, you will be able to understand your need for certain requirements. Often it has to do with vanity but it also has to do with "how you feel about you." You will not allow yourself to wear certain things because of "how you feel about you" and how you feel about your appearance or appearances in general.

When you begin to see how appearances do not count you will feel very foolish. You have lived your entire life on appearances to one degree or another and now I am telling you to not care what anyone says or thinks; not your parents, not your neighbors, not your children and not your teachers. Let go of this need to do what others want you to do. It is peer pressure and it is keeping you from knowing you. You cannot know you because you are so busy trying to please everyone and do what is "right." It is not right just because the majority says so. Right is not right. You are all confused and stuck in ignorance, and what you are teaching is keeping you in ignorance. There is no better way to stay in the dark than by going into agreement with everyone else who is in the dark. Let's have some free thinking here and let's have some independent behavior.

Do not ask permission or seek approval for your thoughts. You have a God given right that is over and beyond anything you have been taught about "rights." This God given right is grace. You are in a state of grace if you will just receive it. You are in grace at all times if you will just acknowledge that you are. Grace is the wisdom of God. Grace is trust and faith. Grace is knowing that all is God. Grace is where you want to be. Grace is the biggest part of you that you are searching for. When you find grace you will never again feel the pain of loss. Grace will tell you how you do not lose, you simply change. Your fear of loss sticks you to one place and your acceptance of grace will lead you gracefully into the next step. Everything is just a step; one foot in front of the other.

You will begin to see that all of you are in a pool and swimming in all directions, and all of you are drowning and asking the others what to do. Stop asking other frantic, panicked, drowning souls what to do. Begin to "know you." Get in touch with you. You have all of the pertinent information right inside of you. Listen to you! Oh, I get it. You don't trust you, but you trust your neighbor because he believes he has the right answers. Well, I suggest that you learn to trust you and to receive all of your answers from you. I know that your schools have taught you to conform and not make waves by being independent thinkers, but what else can unenlightened, unaware souls teach? You can only teach what you believe and you only believe what someone else has taught you. That is unless, just maybe, you have begun to communicate with your own God wisdom. Could it be that you are ready to listen to you? This would be a very good first step for you. Listen to you. Know you. Talk to you. Ask you questions. Open you up. You are God. Get to know you. It is well worth your time and trouble.

For as long as you can remember, you have always had pain and suffering. This is not so much out of necessity as it is out of a desire to see yourself punished for past discrepancies. When you begin to believe that you deserve to be loved, you will end your pain and your struggle. Pain and suffering are due in part to the desire for karmic justice. You believe very strongly in justice and in "getting back at" others for their sins against you, or against those you profess to love. If someone were to kill your child you would go berserk and you would avow to kill them or see them brought to justice. To you this seems like the most natural and "right" thing to do. You have been programmed to see it this way. What if you allowed forgiveness to take the place of justice? What if your child was killed and you said, "Let the man go, he has an agreement with the soul of my child. He kept his agreement."

This is coming from awareness and understanding and it has nothing to do with not caring or not loving your child. It has to do with understanding the soul and its cycle and its bargains, or agreements made, before it ever came into this playing field. You are all playing a big game on this giant playing field, and it is time to give it up and come home. You have gotten too involved and too serious about your game. It was meant to be fun and now you are no longer having fun because you are being self-righteous. When you begin to calm down, your struggle and your pain will begin to calm down. No more suffering and no more judging.

When you learn to accept that you are not in control and even that you do not wish to be in control, you will begin to see a pattern to all of life. You will begin to see how you no longer feel the urge to "get back at" others, no matter how awful they may appear. It just will not be part of your nature to "get back at." Revenge will become a thing of the past and you will flow with whatever is occurring in your daily life.

The interesting thing is that you will not be in your same perspective, so you will no longer see things as unjust and you will not feel it necessary to punish anyone because you will only see good in every situation. How can you seek revenge if you are seeing only good in every situation? Revenge will not have a grip on you and you will have moved into forgiveness, or to be more exact, you will have moved into *acceptance*. Acceptance is a very good place to be. Love and acceptance go hand-in-hand. Once you learn to accept that everything has a purpose and can be clearly understood from a higher level of awareness, you will let go of the need to judge it and fix it and punish it. You will begin to "allow it." This, of course, will take some time yet, as you are very strongly programmed to attack anything that you do not agree with.

As you learn to walk in grace, you will begin to see how you need not carry justice and injustice with you. These serve no purpose and are very destructive to your nature. Your nature is love. Your nature is to play and have fun. Your nature is not to be so serious and to decide who or what is evil. There is no evil so you will let go of this need to create evil. You are now moving into a time that is most conducive to you. This time is a time of integration and healing. It is the healing of you. It is a time when you become whole by bringing your Father/Mother God into balance. You are becoming God. God does not judge. God does not punish and God is not into revenge. Come out of revenge. Let it all go!

When you begin to receive light you will begin to vibrate and to release dark energy that has been trapped and programmed into you. You will begin to see how you not only do not wish to remain in darkness and denial; you do not wish to remain outside the light. The light is very powerful and will have a powerful effect on you. You will know you are in the light when you begin to see your life change. In the beginning you may feel euphoric, and a sense of well-being will raise you to new heights. As the light permeates your total essence you begin to release old patterns and old fears. This may cause you some pain and emotional upheaval as you are literally vibrating your garbage to the surface. As you vibrate your garbage to the surface you will be very much in it and overwhelmed by it at times. *This does not mean that you are bad or wrong.* This simply means that you are healing by moving all of your programming and fear to the surface so you no longer hide in it or allow it to hide in you.

This is not always a comfortable journey and you will see and feel hate, rage, revenge, animosity, fear, pain, suffering and anything else that you carry. Do not lose heart. God is with you and you are walking the path to enlightenment. The path to enlightenment means leaving the dark behind. You cannot be both. You must choose. Do you choose love or do you choose fear? Allow your fear to vanish by giving up your need for it. Allow fear to be put aside and allow love to take over. Love will show you 'you'. Love will show you the truth. Love will show you how you are God. Love does not condemn nor does love judge. You will learn to walk in the light with no pain and you will attract to you only light filled essence. The only reason you attract darkness now is to show you that you do not wish to be dark. You wish to be light, and you wish to share in the light or source that is supplying light.

You will find that your source is not worried about your outcome. Your source does not fear and get upset. You get upset with your source because you feel like you are drowning in your own debris. Release your hold on pain. If you no longer use pain it will leave. If you can make choices for yourself based on your love of self you will no longer require pain to jolt you into position or out of position. This is how you use pain: you do not have enough connection with your own feelings to know what you want. You end up using pain to give you a hefty jolt to move you into a new situation or out of an old situation. You do not use pain wisely and it is overused. You may use its counterpart and move in or out of situations out of joy, and you may use joy as you now use pain. Joy is a very good way to use your energy. Every time you use joy to move you, you will be moving closer to joy. This is also true of pain. Whenever you use pain or illness to move you, you will move closer to pain and illness.

Once you begin to take on light and vibrate your darkness to the surface, you will *see* just how much darkness you carry. You will literally see it as you express it and allow it to leave you. You will know that it is in your past and you will know that you are releasing it so that you might be lighter, but you will also feel it in your physical, mental and emotional bodies. This may create some concern for you, but I want you to remember that when you clean house and begin to sweep up dirt and dust that has been storing up, you often need to cover your eyes and nose and mouth. You get it all over you as you clean house. It is not coming in, it is going out! It still sticks to you and it still makes a mess. Have trust and know what you are doing. Know that you are cleaning house and that when this task is complete you will feel much better, and you will actually have a very clean home for the very first time in eons.

You have never before set your goal so high as you are now. You have never before decided to evolve and take all parts of you with you. You have never before decided to transform, while in body, to God light. You have never before agreed to become the birthing canal of God. You are bringing in God and God's way is being prepared. Love is ultimate and love is being born. Love is the ultimate light vibration and love will set you all free. You are birthing love and you are feeling this birthing process at various stages.

Do not be afraid. You are not literally dying. You only are if you wish. Parts of you are dying to make way for the new body that will be made up of cellular memory that you "consciously" gave yourself. No more old ways that were programmed by those who came to live and leave after a fair exchange of time and energy. Now you are coming in and taking the lid off so that you can let some of the steam out of this dimension. It was never meant to be a boiling pot of fear and struggle. It is now being transformed by your very existence in it. If you take on light, you automatically take it on in this dimension and it therefore affects this dimension. It will no longer be in darkness when enough light has been let in.

Once enough light has been let in, it will begin to rise up just as you are now rising up. You do not know it yet, but you are. You have raised your level of understanding and you have released enough to raise your vibration. You are light workers in that you bring in light by your ability to ignite your own system. You are a spark that is being ignited in order to raise your level of awareness. When you rise, everything rises with you.

When you begin to live in the light you will begin to see how good and how easy your life can be. As you begin to live your life from the perspective that you are from a source greater than yourself and you are part of that greatness, you will be more inclined to greatness. You will see how you are a Supreme Being and how you may uncover the truth that is your nature. As you begin to "unfold" and know your true identity, fear will simply become part of your past. You will begin to feel as though you are young again and you never had a care or a problem in the world. All programmed fear will be replaced by "love." Love will take over, and with love come freedom and trust. Trust will bring you into a state of grace, and grace will allow you to continue to flow in the steady current of the powerful source.

As you begin to learn your own nature you will be in a state of confusion. Learning your nature is not the same as discovering your programmed behavior. Your nature is your natural state of being while your programming is who you are taught to be. It is time to discover the real you and to know that you are no longer stuck being what you were taught to be. You may switch over to who you are naturally, and leave the façade behind with the fear that surrounds it. You are moving into that part of you that is more natural and lies beyond the denial and pretense. Honesty of self will attract honesty to you. You will find that, as you become more and more honest within yourself about who and what you are, you will draw like honesty from others. You will begin to unmask others simply by your ability to unmask yourself.

As you return to your natural state you will begin to feel more comfortable being you. You will begin to see how you no longer fear others because you are no longer fearing unknown parts of yourself. You will also begin to know how you will rise to a level of natural beingness that will assist others in their rise also. You do affect one another and you do belong in the same giant source. You are all the body of God and you are all connected to one another and you all belong here together. No one is "less than" and no one is really "different than." It is simply another game that you are playing.

When you begin to "realize" the power of natural living you will choose it over the pretense that has kept you entertained for so long. You will begin to feel more aware of your own likes and dislikes, and you will begin to know that you are developing into a slimmer version of yourself. You will have trimmed down the fat and left only the lean parts. You will have kept the stuff that was truly your nature and the rest you will have let go of. You will learn to walk through life with a positive attitude simply because you will know who you really are. You will no longer be searching for your answers because you will know you, and you will no longer have questions regarding "why this" or "why not that." When you leave the fake part of you behind you begin to develop into what is left. Only the essence that is you has any validity. The rest of you has no place in you and is programmed nonsense.

You are coming alive now and you are being born as your own true self. You will like this new you as she/he emerges. Do not worry, death of the old brings birth and new life. You are just now coming into you and you are very much real when you are in your body. As you begin to allow more parts of you to come alive you will begin to see how you no longer fear what is outside of you, as you will be totally "in" you and what is outside will be only the projected image of what once was.

You will gradually begin to see a change in the way the outside world responds to you as you begin to see how you are responding differently to the outside world. Love begets love and fear begets fear. When you know yourself and walk "in" yourself you will be liking who you are. This liking will quickly change to loving and all will fall into place. Love is that place. All life will be love and you will have reached your state of happiness or "heaven brought down to earth."

You will begin to see how you are no longer one of many who seek to destroy their own good. You will begin to allow pleasure and you will begin to know that your pleasure is part of your nature. As you begin to allow all parts of you to be served by your true nature you will be among those who walk in peace. You will find that as you walk into joy you begin to discover peace. Peace is very much a part of your nature and peace is very much a part of you. When you chose chaos and warlike ways you all but destroyed the peacefulness that you once felt. When you regain your peaceful ways you will no longer be full of anger and warlike emotions. You will become patient and calm. You will become serene and you will have peace within. Peace within will draw peace without, and you will find that you no longer get involved in news reports concerning war and violence and chaos. It simply will not concern you. I know this sounds strange to you now and that you are *programmed* to "be concerned" about everything, but this too shall change.

You will begin to see a new phase of your life open up for you, and you will begin to see how you can use your own peacefulness to create greater calm and tranquility in your world. It is all a matter of perspective, really. In the same way that you do not get upset and involved when your little child comes running in to tattle on the four year old next door who just did a big no-no, you will listen and be patient but you will not get all upset because you know that the child is simply playing and learning. You are all children playing in learning. Now you are learning peace instead of war and violence. Now you are learning love of self instead of self-loathing and self-discipline. Now you are learning to do for you and to care for you instead of handing you over to another. Now you are learning to grow and expand within instead of closing off and shutting down within. Now you are learning to be whole instead of pushing part of you away. You are learning to love and accept you and to no longer fear and reject you.

You are coming together quite nicely and you will be very good to live with. You will live with you and in you because you have come into balance enough to remain and not push your other half out. You are learning to accept and allow negative/positive within the self. You are learning to come out of denial and to own, and often allow movement in, all parts of you. You are growing in wholeness which allows for peace and balance to enter your life. You have reached a place of great self-acceptance and you will continue to accept more and more of you. You will require maintenance and this will be easy enough. A good diet and fresh water, a good self image and gratitude for yourself, and an enema a day will keep you in balance and out of fearful ways.

Your food is your gas so keep it clean and natural. Your thoughts are your projection onto your world so keep them pleasing, and your body is your only way to experience in the now, so treat it as though it were a king. Give you love. Give you praise. Give you gentle thoughts and give you to you. Don't be giving yourself away to others. You are the gold ring and very valuable. Those of you who have touched your emotional bodies and released old, pent-up "charge" will realize how valuable a clear body can be. You have seen the amount of fear that can be released, and you will value you all the more for that gift that you have so unselfishly bestowed on yourself. It is good to know you and it is good to let go of the past by acknowledging it instead of trying to bury it or simply deny it.

You will find that as you come into balance you will have come full circle and you will begin to feel young again. You will find yourself full of energy and you will find yourself enjoying life in a much fuller capacity than ever before. You will find that as you begin to move from pain to pleasure you will begin to know your own self in an entirely different way. You have always known struggle and pain. Now we will see how you do with peace and pleasure. You may find it difficult at first to accept since you are so accustomed to the opposite. Do not worry. You will learn to love and depend on pleasure just as much as you have learned to depend on pain. You will no longer be afraid of getting what you want and you will no longer fear that your "reach for the stars" will result in disappointment. When you reach for the stars now you will not have your old programming that shouts, "You can't have that. You're not good enough." You will not deal with the part of you who hated you because that part just came back to you and you embraced it and welcomed it home. You did this by accepting and loving and bringing out of the darkness all of your true feelings and motivations.

You are growing to discover that you have more beauty and greatness in you than anyone has ever conveyed to you. No one, not even you, told you how you are God. No one told you how you are the creator of your life and how you could do it any way that you wish. You may now teach yourself and, in doing so, you will be allowing yourself to grow and expand as the creator God. You are God. You are love and you are loved. You are not to be put down or walked on or stomped on or shut out. Do not do this to yourself and do not allow this treatment from others. You are going to dream big and you must allow you to dream big. You are changing and growing. God is growing *in* you and you are becoming what is growing in you. It is not separate from you. You are God and God is in you. You are God and you are in God. God is you and is in you. God is you and you are one; whole; complete.

When you begin to feel this wholeness and this completeness you will be able to accomplish all that you wish for. Your priorities may change and your needs may disappear, but you will still have your dreams, and your creative ability will be freer than ever to create what you require to arrive at your dreams. You will receive as you have never before. You will know yourself as never before. You will be in balance as never before and you will love you as never before. Out of that love will come a bright and joyous union with your own God and your own image and your own identity. Out of that love will come peace and wisdom and a newfound kindness toward yourself and toward others. You will love all as all love will come from you and through you and back again. You will become your own source and you will be God.

God is becoming in this three-dimensional time and space. God is coming in and taking over. God is taking over you. You have little time left. God is here. God is now and God is within you. You are transforming and you know it. This awareness will assist you in knowing how to handle your discomfort at times. You are being born. God is being born. Creation was never complete until the creator entered his/her creation. You are now entering and you are becoming all that you can be. You will be operating in full swing soon.

As you grow in your ability to take on light you will begin to see how your light is shining. You are actually beginning to shine and to glow. This attracts "those who want light" to you. This also attracts "those who are already taking on light" to you. You will begin to see how you are not only not being rejected you will be totally received because you are totally receiving you. You are living in you and you are happy to be you and, therefore, you create happiness and joy around you. This happens automatically and you can begin to see how all life will change when you have changed. You are being forced to change because you did not like you. You are becoming love and allowing fear to fall away, in order to create space for you to be in love with you. All the world loves love. You will radiate love and this will be very attractive. The laws of attraction simply state that like attracts like. You will begin to see how you are no longer in a state of repulsion simply because you are accepting and owning all parts of you.

As you begin to attract "like" to you, you will also begin to see how you have changed by noting how you attract or draw to you. You will begin to see how you are moving within your own self and allowing parts of you to be free while discarding old unnecessary ideas and rules and laws that you once used to protect yourself. As you begin to move into your most basic nature you will see great changes occur. Your most basic nature does not rule over others and it does not pay homage to others. Your most basic nature is well "aware" of who you are and so it will allow you to be equal with everyone and it will allow everyone to be equal with you.

When you begin to see this type of balance return to your life you will know that you are beginning to get in touch with your basic self. Your true nature or true identity is beginning to shine through. As your true nature shines through, you will become very happy and very much in love with who you are. Your true nature is the essence that pours forth from the source and has established itself as you. You are essence and your identity is God sent. You will create according to your beliefs or disbeliefs, and when I can get you to release your grip on all the rules and allow you to be free and stop judging yourself, you will also be free to stop judging others. You will be free to know you and you will be free to know God. You will no longer hide God behind a façade of ideas and half-baked truths. You will begin to see God for his/her true essence which is love and total acceptance. How can such a God have rules? It makes no sense.

You are now in a position to become a more dynamic part of your own nature. You are rising up out of your programming and your beliefs, and you are creating a new you by your ability and need to rise up above duality and negativity. You will begin to rise and allow others to rise, or to stay, or to lower. It is all God creating and it does not matter. It simply does not matter. So; if you want to feel better by moving you, you can. If you want to feel the same as you always have about you, you can. If you want to feel worse, you can. It's all up to you. You are God creating in matter and you may create it anyway you want it.

You will begin to discover that not only do you wish for light in your life, you also wish for divine intervention. In some cases this is possible, in others it is not. When you receive divine intervention you may not recognize it. This is due to the fact that you all want certain things in your life and you expect your life to run a certain way or you will not accept it as adequate. What if God's idea of what is good does not coincide with your idea of what is good? What if God intervenes and you are moved spiritually to a place that is meant to show you how you have grown, and you are afraid that you are not in your right place or that you will get hurt or lost in the scheme of things?

You are never sure of what God wants for you because you never ask God. You are never aware of God's intentions, because you do not ask what God wants or how God wishes to view reality. You constantly focus from within limitation and this limits you. I want you to begin to ask God how to live and to ask God what he/she wants of you. Begin to see God as your highest essence, and you will be asking your own intelligence or wisdom for advice.

When you begin to communicate with God in this way, you will be raising your own consciousness up to a level of intelligence that is conducive to the flow that you are communicating with. You will be seeing all parts of your own information center as one big communications center. You will connect with God on high and you will communicate with God/you. When you begin to communicate with God intelligence, it is best to remain calm and to know that you are actually connected to and part of God. So, why shouldn't everyone and anyone connect with that part of themselves and communicate freely with that part? You are mostly here to learn to express for God, so it stands to reason that you would at least be in some form of communication with God.

Do not be afraid to face God and to speak with God directly. Most of you are so programmed to have a priest or rabbi or minister or pastor do the work for you. You have decided that you are not good enough or just too busy, so you go to someone else to find out what God wants. If God is inside of you, how can you not be the one to communicate directly with God? You are in God just as the head of the church or religion is in God. You are God and God is you. Why must you go anywhere to receive God or communicate with God? That is all ceremony and it simply does not take precedence over you sitting at home and talking with God. God is everywhere and can be communicated with at any time in any place.

As you reach out to God you will actually be reaching "in" to God. I know you raise your eyes up to heaven when you address God but he's/she's actually everywhere. God does not exist in any one place and God does not react in any one way. I want you to stop teaching that you must live your life a certain way in order to receive

God. You need not act this way or that way and you need not ask for forgiveness to receive God. God "is" and you "are." Everyone is God – not just he/she but everyone and everything. You are God and everything you see and do not see is God. You will find that you cannot go outside of God and that God takes up all that is. God is the creator and he is the creation, and he is she, and he is it, and he is nothing. He is the entire spectrum from nothing to everything and he is every gender and form from human to rock energy. God is not limited but you must limit God because you live in limited thought.

You must begin to receive yourself as God in order to receive light. Light is what you are hungry for and once you begin to feel the light you will want more of it. You will become very attracted to the light and you will grow and revel in it. The light has been waiting to receive you since the beginning. The light is all things and the light will heal all things. Allow yourself to go with the flow of source and source will take you to light. Source always returns to light.

You may begin to feel that you are not part of God and that you are not part of anything. This is you "disconnecting" in order to flow. Once you have disconnected, you will begin to move into position to flow into the source and out of the muck and mire of the past. You are always in the source, but do not move when you are stuck to the bottom like heavy mud in a stream. As you begin to lighten, you will begin to open up to all possibilities, and one of those possibilities is that you will speak freely with God at any given moment. No ritual or knee bending or heavy meditation is required. Simply say, "God – are you here" and God will be. God always is. Let the voice speak back to you. Do not be afraid to hear the voice of God. Do not stop it when it speaks. It will sound like you or it may sound totally different than you. It all depends on what you can accept.

When you learn to listen to the voice of God, begin to ask God what God wants and how God is seeing things. You just may be very surprised with what God has to say. After all, you are God and you never knew you were until just recently. Now it is time to discover even more about your God/self relationship. No intermediaries or priests or channels; just you and God in a nice cozy conversation. What a nice idea!

You will begin to see how you are turning your life over to the light when you begin to feel this giant shift that will take place in you. You are transforming and a great deal of change is taking place within you. As you begin your change, you will see how you are no longer stuck and yet you are confused about who you are and what is occurring. You are moving into the center of you and this takes a great deal of movement on your part. Your desire for light has begun to shift you into position to take on light.

After you begin to receive light you will have time to digest your new position, or stay in you. You will be given the time that is required to stay and absorb the light that will frighten you. Some can only take light in very small doses and must not be shocked into a state of greater mistrust of the light. You will find that most of you are not only being put in a position to take on light, you are also in a position to see happiness. You, however, do not know how to do either. You are so accustomed to seeing the negative side of life that you are not allowing yourself to see or to look for the good in all things.

As you begin to look for the good, you will begin a very subtle shift in the direction of the good that you have seen. If you continually look for or focus on what you do not like, it will overwhelm you and it will take up all your conscious thought. Begin to see what you like, and focus on it until you can begin to see it in everything. Everything serves a purpose and everything gives out a vibration. If you push at a vibration you actually do a dance with it. If you leave a vibration alone you will not get involved and no dance occurs. So if you want stuff to stick to you or dance with you, reach out and touch it. If you don't want to get it on you, do not get involved with it. If you think you like it, and you do a dance or two only to discover it is no longer what you want, you may let go of it and move on. Not everything is meant to be a commitment and not everything is meant to stick.

When you learn how to flow, you will better understand how commitment and non-commitment work. You need not promise your allegiance to anyone or anything. You only flow with the source and you do not owe your energy to anyone else. They have their own attachments and their own direct connection to source. Why would you have to take care of their emotional needs if they are connected to God? Some of you are playing the role of being connected while others are playing dumb. Some pretend to not be able to live without others, and this is due to the confusion about love and commitment and meeting one's needs by using another's energy. You will find that you no longer require commitment when you all reach the light. Commitment sticks you in one place and it implies that you have promised so you must stick it out, or continue to stick to it.

Once you begin to see how you are being led into commitments that you don't really want, you will begin to change. You commit to everything from signing contracts for house payments or contracts for car payments to contracts for living with one another. You are "binding" yourself up in agreement. I want you to flow. If God says "get up and move" how can you with all these contracts "holding you" back? Now; I know you live in a world full of contracts and commitments, but I just want you to know that there is a much more productive and an easier way. It is unheard of today but it will be the cornerstone of your lives in the future. It is called "trust." Nothing else; just trust! "God will provide" will be well accepted and received in the future, and you will no longer live in a world of mistrust and a belief in lack. And everything will have come full circle and you will know that you are no longer "stuck." You will be "free" to flow.

When you begin to discover that you are indeed shifting consciousness you will begin to see changes in your perception as well as your logic. When you begin to shift your perception you may let go of logic altogether or you may find that you no longer consider yourself logical. You may begin also to know that you are blessed in certain areas of your life, and it is not necessary to question how you received the gifts that you have received. When you begin to see how you are always being hurt by your own rejection of good, you will begin to see how you are also very limited in your flow.

Once you get the flow moving, you will be much closer to receiving from the flow. You will learn to raise your level of awareness to the extent that you will receive and not block. This is not a technique and it is not a trick. You do not learn tricks to manifestation. I know you are learning to manifest millions and to have a successful business, but this will last only as long as you can get around your own subconscious programming. Why not wait until you shift consciousness and then simply *allow* the prosperity to flow. There will be no struggle and no pain. Just become all that you can be by letting go of all that blocks you. You may not wish to wait, as it may take a little time. You may decide to go ahead and manifest as you are.

In this case you will still achieve your goal. The only benefit to waiting until you are clear is that you will be able to flow with your manifestation and not against it. You will work with it to nurture it and not destroy it. Do you have destructive tendencies? Do you tend to destroy the good that you create?

These are not necessarily the only problems with your own ability to have what you want. They are, however, very strong in inhibiting the inflow of good and the outflow of good. If you are taking in good you are usually giving out good. When you begin to see how you are not taking in what is felt as good, you will wish to change to what feels good. As you change to what feels good you begin to shift into a greater acceptance of self, and with this acceptance comes a greater ease of movement. Everything will begin to flow and everything will begin to simply "ease" into place.

As you learn to manifest from this state of being, you will become aware of your consciousness and what part it plays in receiving. Most of what you are receiving is brought forward by both conscious and unconscious behavior. Most of you know what you want on a conscious level but you are totally unaware of what your subconscious is programming and creating. This is what we are clearing and this is what will destroy it if it is not conducive to your own subconscious needs. "It" can be anything from a new car to a new relationship or a new job. You will "get it" and "love it" and "lose it" if your subconscious programming is powerfully built in the "destroy" area.

When you begin to realize how you are programmed, you can then readjust your own mindset by convincing yourself that you *are* lovable and you do deserve. As long as you continue to believe that you are guilty on some level, you will continue to punish yourself by taking things away from you. You are innocent and everyone else walking this planet is innocent. If you find them guilty and offensive it is just a reflection of how you find yourself guilty and offensive. You are seeing yourself in everyone. You can measure your own trust or mistrust by how you trust or mistrust others and life. You are full of programming from pain – "do not do this, it is painful. Do not do that, it will harm you."

You will find that, as you begin to come into your unconscious behavior, you will begin to see a big part of you that has been "in charge" for a very long time. This is this part that carries a great deal of negative charge and negative response to life situations. As with everything else this part of you once had a purpose and it was to keep you "in balance." This part of you is now so negatively charged that it cannot release charge fast enough to keep up with incoming charge.

You are hurting and harming you in ways that you never believed or dreamed of before. This is to fulfill the desire for pain that is now in place in you. You have created a void where pleasure once resided and you have filled it with pain. Now it attracts more and more pain to it. You are beginning to move into balance if you are doing your enema. Enema releases and discharges ions that carry an electrical message. The charge is the message. The imbalanced ion could be positive or negative and it could cause pain or pleasure sensations. Your pain is so out of control that most pleasure is brief, or is drowned in its own discharge before it ever surfaces into consciousness. You are being drowned in your own pain as well.

This is the time of rising up out of this drowning situation. You are going to rise above past programming and become all that is truly you. You are going to balance and you are going to find that your life will flow smoothly and easily. It is no longer necessary to live and to create from pain. Pleasure is your true state and you just got off track and out of balance for a while. You are no longer going to be so out of balance, and your life will no longer be so much one way or the other. You are now going to ride in the middle. No left or right is necessary. You will find your balance and you will give up the "up and down" ride you have been on for so long. This is how you find your center. You will be much happier once you do and you will no longer need excitement and its lows. You will find balance and its ease.

When you begin to see how you are now merging with all consciousness you will begin to know that you are indeed becoming part of the source. This source is very powerful and you have tried to avoid it for a very long time. When you open to the source you begin to allow it to flow through you and to become part of you. You are also becoming aware of this pattern of energy movement. Energy is meant to flow and to move. Energy is meant to be in place one moment and moving on the next. Energy is what gives life to everything. It is not only 'not' your job to stop energy it is not your job to interfere with its path.

When energy shifts it is part of the greater consciousness. It is part of the cycle that is created when energy moves. When you interfere with the flow, you are creating changes that are not "natural" or "in the nature of" undirected energy. Energy is not meant to be directed by limitation. Once energy is given over to the ultimate source it becomes all encompassing, and it returns to the source to reinsure correct patterns and events. Energy is not only 'not' your divine right, it was not meant for you to destroy. You got a little carried away and thought that you might begin to change and control, to the extent that you bottlenecked energy and now you are blocked and it is blocked. You will learn to flow with creation and not always bend everything to your will, especially now that you realize just how limited your perspective on things can be.

So; as you begin to learn how to merge with the source, you will also be merging with creation and not judging how it is. You will be creating a safe place for you to enter creation instead of clearing out everything (that you do not want) for your own benefit. Once you begin to realize how much you are learning to flow, you will wish to be free of any manipulation of energy. Energy is one of the many things you have decided to take charge of, and manipulation does not necessarily mean that you are wrong in what you do; it just means that things might work smoother without it.

You are moving into a new phase of consciousness and you are beginning to become one of the doorways in which consciousness might enter creation. As you move into new areas, or new phases, you will begin to see how you no longer wish to be stuck in energy that is not flowing. To flow you must receive and release whenever necessary. To flow you must be transparent enough that you do not block energy. Transparency is very close to nothingness, and the less you are, the more accessible you are to the light. The denser or thicker you are the less accessible you are.

As you move into a position of knowing and out of a position of not knowing, you will have the awareness required to allow you the choices that are for your own spiritual growth. As you review your learning, I wish you to remember that you are changing by the simple fact that you are reading information that may cause a *shift* in consciousness. This is energy shifting and beginning to move. You are energy and you are moving and growing. You are expanding, and you are turning your energy towards your understanding which is increasing. When you have become unblocked you will begin to run energy through new parts of you that were not working and shut down. This is the opening up of you and it will allow the source to connect with you and begin to surge through you.

When you begin to surge you will begin to know the power of reconnecting with your source. This connection will enable you to rise up out of limitation and lack. This connection will allow you to create from source and to move towards the source. Like attracts like and the light will move to the light. Stay light. You are beginning to move to the light now.

As you begin to merge with the light you will begin to see change in your behavior. You will no longer require, nor will you demand, control over situations. You will flow with situations and your life will flow with you. When you reach this point you will begin to see how you are coming together with your most important part. You will literally be merging with the essence that is you. You have always known that there was a part of you that did not get upset and did not require control to feel safe, and this is that part. It is the part of you who is God. God is in you and working through you and you are part of God.

As you merge into this part of you, your life will seem to take on a life of its own. Your life will flow from one situation to the next, and you will feel as though you have been put in place to receive pieces of information or to receive pieces of yourself. The more whole and complete that you become the more 'here' you are. As you retrieve all lost parts of the self by accepting and allowing yourself to be, you will come full circle back to yourself. You will totally accept *all* of you and you will therefore be accepting God because God is you. There are many parts of you that you have denied in the past, and to know you and how you work is the greatest gift you can give to yourself.

As you begin to learn more and more about your own place and how you fit in, you will begin to feel as though you are part of something very grand. You will no longer feel as though you are separate and alone. You will become aware of all who surround you and all who are not seen in your dimension. There are many, many parts of you and they do not all "appear" in this dimension. When you begin to see how you are everywhere at once, you will know how you are far greater than even you realize.

As your consciousness begins to shift, you may continue to be your old self or you may develop into an entirely different personality. You may change so drastically that your friends comment on your change. It is also possible to become so happy with your own choices that even you are amazed at the change you see in you. As you continue to change and merge with the light, you will begin to see certain patterns of behavior fall by the wayside. You will be discarding those habits and patterns which no longer serve you. You will also see big changes in your "needs." Your needs will no longer feel like needs. You will switch from feeling like you "need" something to feeling like you "might like to have" something. This is a big change and not nearly so desperate. This, of course, is due to the fact that you have connected to the flow.

When you have connected and merged with the light, you will begin to see how you no longer are afraid and alone. You are no longer separate and you no longer feel the need to struggle. When you let go of your need for struggle you will have moved into a very unique position. Think of life without struggle. You will be creating only the best for you without pain, because you have no longer any *need* for pain. You know now that you are innocent of any wrongdoing, because you simply let go of your good guy/bad guy theory. You know that you have committed no offenses to God, so there is no need for punishment or retaliation.

Once you have totally absorbed this truth and let go of your need to punish you, you will begin to let go of your struggle. Your struggle against all odds and your struggle against pain was actually your struggle against you and your need to draw punishment to you for your past sins. There are no sins and you are now free to be totally innocent and totally free of pain and punishment and judgment. You have begun with a clean slate and you have a lifetime of living in the light to catch up on. Enough of the darkness – you are walking out into the light of a new day and you are beginning to know that you are part of God.

As you learn to let go of more clutter and debris from past lives and past programming, you will be allowing yourself to set a new standard of living that is more conducive to "light" thinking. This new standard will be simple. It will be an acceptance of everything with the wisdom that divine order is always taking place and every step we take is to lead us out of darkness. Sometimes you have to go back and face your demons so that you might release them. This is how you are being led out of your dark side and into your love. As you look into your dark side you will know that you are simply looking at a part of you that you had hidden out of shame and guilt. It is okay to allow this part of you to merge with God. This part of you is love as well as the rest of you. You just did not think that this part of you was acceptable to God and so you shoved it into the bottom of you. With enema, even the bottom of you gets to release itself.

You are cleaning out and cleaning up you so that you might begin again. You need not kill you out of disgust and distaste for who or what you are. You need not sicken you to death with illness you can't even name, and you need not kill you off in an accident. Let you live, and let God walk hand-in-hand with you as you begin to see the glory of the way and the gift of light that you truly are. You will find yourself truly in a state of love and unconditional forgiveness of self when you have let go of the myth that has been spreading for eons. This myth says that God punishes you for bad... God does not. This myth says that God does not accept half-truths... there is no such thing. This myth says that you are beneath God... you are "in" God. And this myth says that you are not deserving of God's love... you are God and his love is you.

You will find that as you grow closer and closer to God by allowing you to be God and by allowing God to be you, you will begin to notice two things. God is a nice guy and you are a nice guy (or gal – whichever). You are both nice and you are both in each other so I suggest you begin to get along. You are learning to merge and to form a bond. God and you are bonding. God and you are becoming "one." God and you are becoming friends. You and God are beginning to love you by your acceptance of God and your acceptance of you. You can push God out of your life by not accepting God, or you can allow God in by acceptance and end the battle within for once and for all. God is love and you have always pushed God away out of fear that you are not good enough. Love comes in when you say, "Okay, I'm good enough."

As you begin to see your own shortcomings and your own fears, you will have a tendency to judge and manipulate and control yourself. Try to remember that nothing is wrong with you. There is no wrong way; there are only choices to be made. If you can remember this you will not be so hard on yourself. You do not dwell on how bad you are when you remember how you are divine God expression. How can you be so horrible if God is expressing through you?

You will begin to see how you not only do not belong in self-condemnation; you also do not wish the punishment that usually follows self-condemnation. You are part of the plan and you do not remember what the plan is, so now you judge and condemn and try to punish yourself and others for not being this way or that way. You are beginning to see how you are the plan in action, and you are connected to all that is good and holy. So, if you are connected to it, how can you not be good and holy? Just because you do not see yourself as good and holy does not mean that you are not. It also does not mean that you are what you see yourself as.

When God began to separate and to move and to change, he did not expect huge parts to begin to feel outside of God. It's as if you get up and begin to walk only to find your shoes have "fallen" off. You did not mean for your shoes to fall off, it is simply a "result" of walking. This sometimes occurs and is no big thing unless you are the shoes and you begin to feel left out and left behind. You will find that as you begin to be more aware you will notice more parts that you have left behind. As you notice what has been dropped off or left behind, you may decide to retrieve certain parts for yourself. You may have a good use for these parts and you may find them very helpful in your quest to make you whole.

As you rediscover these parts that fell off from the exertion of moving forward, you will begin to see how you once were part of everything and you once knew everything. You now know very little and are part of your world but feel separate and disconnected. When you begin to reconnect, you will begin to see how you were once part of everything. This may frighten you as you are not yet certain that you wish to be everything – even though you already are!

As you begin to move from where you now stand to the awareness that awaits you, you will feel a certain pull to return and hide in your separateness. Do not fear. This is a natural reaction considering your state of unnatural behavior. Once I move you into the source and you begin to return to your natural essence, you will feel very comfortable at the thought of being everything. When you begin to see how you are no longer separate, and you actually begin to merge with God and source and self, you will find it totally overwhelming at times. At other times you will find it as natural as breathing in and breathing out. You will begin to know that you are your own creator, and you will begin to know that each individual is exactly as you are. You are all the same, from the bottom of the gutter to the top of your royalty list. You simply prefer some and shun others. You may meet someone who has opposite tastes and choices. They may love what you hate and hate what you love. It is only a choice and it means little if anything.

So, as you begin to know how you are everything, I do hope you will remember that your neighbor is too. You are all the same. Do not be offended by looking upon you. Some of you create big messes to show the rest of you what you are doing. Others create big traumas to show you how you are acting, and still others show you your own vulnerability and your own fear. You are all the same so why not stop complaining about your neighbor, or just get on with "awareness" and "enlightenment." Don't judge lest ye be judged and don't "point fingers at" lest the finger turn to you. You are all that is here. You live in you and you feel in you. If you feel it, it affects you, not your neighbor. Your revenge runs through you and your resentment runs through you. Get it together and know what you are doing when you judge and condemn either yourself or another.

When you begin to surrender to the source, you will begin to see how your life flows with ease and with grace. You will be moving along on a current that will take you through your life as never before. You will begin to feel as though everything just works "for" you and nothing seems to disturb the flow. You will learn to accept what comes and to allow yourself to receive more than you ever thought possible. This will be a receiving of joy and love and all that is conducive to your spiritual requirements. As you begin to feed and nurture your spiritual requirements you will be giving directly to your soul. You will be giving to you on a new level. As you learn to give more and more to yourself you will also be giving more and more to God. As a matter of fact this is a very good way to give to God. All that you give to you, you give to God and since God is you it is a double gift.

When you begin to learn to live within the spirit as well as the body, you will begin to feel certain changes take place within you. You will begin to feel uncertain, as this is an uncertain and new place for you to be, and you will begin to feel as though something is going to happen for you but you just don't know what. This is expectation based on new hope for a new future. You are changing who you are, and as you do so you begin to change who you will be. This will affect your future as well as your past, and it will also affect your direct and even indirect lives which are running parallel to this particular life. As you begin to set into motion a new pattern of living and thinking, you will be affecting everyone and everything in creation. As this chain reaction begins to build momentum things will begin to get easier for everyone. Since you are part of this chain reaction your life will then become easier and more fluid. In this way you get to see how you are both the cause and the effect.

You begin the movement by agreeing to change and when the movement has grown big enough to affect everyone, you get affected too. What you began went full circle and came back to you and others. This is how creation works. You all think it and then project it, then you view it and allow it to return. On its return it begins to touch other thoughts and moves in and out of each of them. It then either dies out from the overriding of other thoughts, or it begins to blend in and create more of itself as it picks up momentum. This is the cycle of creation, and it is how energy moves and shifts and blends and changes to create new worlds based on new thought. Your next world will be a world of peace and joy and love and it will flow with grace. It will no longer require pain and punishment for it will not be based on judgment. It will be based on unconditional love.

As you begin to move into this new world, you may not require some of the baggage you now carry. This is the most difficult part for you! You are so afraid to give up your baggage and your addictions. You are so afraid to give up your pain. You will find that as you begin to learn how to surrender, you will also learn that surrender is something you can fight or you can flow with. The choice is yours, and the pain of fighting will exhaust you just as quickly as anything. So you might as well just surrender and let it all go now rather than fight until you are exhausted. But I'll let you choose as I always have.

You will begin to see how you no longer wish to remain connected to certain people in the way that you have been connected. Often you find people to nurture you and sometimes you look for those who will give you light. You are your own source of light and you are being put in a position to depend on that source. As you grow in light you will begin to see how you are not only 'not' the only one who is searching for light, you are also not the only one who has forgotten his or her direct connection. Once you begin to reconnect, you may begin to know more about you. As you reconnect with source you will be opening a part of you that is all knowing and very wise. You will learn to look to yourself for guidance and direction, and you will learn to look to God to be more and more a part of you.

As you begin to leave old parts of you behind, you will be learning that you are beginning to enter your future with less of you. You will leave behind the shame and guilt that have kept you locked behind giant walls of protection. You will leave behind many parts of you that you no longer wish to carry because of their density. When you leave these parts behind, you will find that you become "lighter" in more ways than you can imagine. You will literally begin to flow through life. This is not to be taken as a muse. You do not feel drugged out and unassociated with life, but you do feel a certain peace and comfort with life. Life will no longer be pushing and threatening for you. You will no longer be put upon and pushed at to perform, because the one who put upon and pushed at you was you. Your own programming has taught you to bully your own self. This will end when you let go of guilt and shame.

You are now at a very big turning point, and you are learning to recognize your own programming and to own it so that you might change it. If you do not own it you will not be able to recognize it for what it is. When you own it you can then say, "No thank you. I don't need this anymore." As you begin to leave behind what you no longer wish to burden yourself with, you will begin to feel less burdened and much freer to express your true nature which is love. As you begin to express love, you will also begin to love you. Your expression is you and you are what you express. So, as love comes to the surface you will begin to love everyone and everything. This love is, of course, acceptance and has little to do with the "desire" to have or own one another.

When love begins to take over it is so strong it literally vibrates and sends out signals. When you are in a state of projecting love it is felt by everyone. You radiate from within and you do this with little or no thought. It simply "is." When you learn to simply allow this process, without being concerned that you might get hurt or harmed or upset, you will be allowing God free reign to express in your life. God expresses love and does not wish to express guilt and shame any longer. You have done guilt and shame for so long that you are very stuck in it. You are not only 'not' being honest when you play in guilt and shame, you are also not being loving. Your true essence goes right out the door and you begin to get lost in the shame that you yourself are projecting. This shame was, of course, taught to you and projected onto you until you knew it well. Now it is time to change. Now it will be love that is projected onto you until you know it well.

As you begin to walk in love and to know your own capacity for love, you will be receiving your own in-depth fulfillment. You will begin to focus on joy and peace as never before, and your height of joy will constantly increase and spread to every area of your life. Life will become joyful. Your work will no longer feel burdensome and you will find joy in even the most mundane task. The burden of guilt and sorrow will have been lifted, and you will rejoice in the wisdom of knowing that you are not only unstuck and flowing with your source, you are also unstuck and moving into love. It will be good to be *in* love after such a long bout with fear. Love and fear are merging, and as this occurs you will feel the darkness slip away as the new dawn brings forth light, and with the light comes love and compassion.

As you begin to see the light for the first time it will be foreign to you. You have always hidden from the light to hide your shame. Now you will face the light and know that you are light and have no need for shame. You will begin to see how shame has forced you down on your knees, and you will see how shame has driven you from God, which is your own self. You were driven by you from the Garden of Eden by your own belief in your guilt. Now God is telling you that there is no guilt. There is no shame and no one did anything wrong. If you can believe that, then you will allow yourself to return to the Garden of Eden to live out your lives in joy and peace.

You have always been separated from God by your belief that you did wrong. There is no wrong and God could care less about the theft of an apple from a tree. No one steals and no one dies. You are playing games with yourselves, and it is time to come out of this game and return home. You are hiding you from God and now it is time to show you to God.

When you begin to move into the light you will find that you no longer fear being God. Your greatest fear has always been that you are God. You do not wish to be God because you do not wish to accept that you create it all. You do not wish to accept that you create it all, because you judge "all" to the extent that you have guilt and shame. When you begin to see how you no longer wish to judge it as bad, or awful, or not good, or wrong, you will begin to see peace. You will find peace with God and you will find peace in love. When you can accept everything without condemning it you will have come full circle. You will be in God where you began. You actually never left but, to you, it feels like you did so this is how I will describe it. You are now in a position to put down judgment and to accept that you are God. God does not care to judge nor does God care to dole out punishment. This is all your creation and it is your way of hiding from yourself. When you begin to know yourself you will begin to know how much you have hidden from you.

When you begin to uncover certain areas of consciousness within your greater consciousness, you will begin to expand and to grow. More of you will come in to fill the space that has been provided by this expansion. As more of you comes in to take residence "in" you, you will begin to feel more and more whole. You will not feel so lonely and you will not feel so separated from the rest of you. As bigger and bigger gaps are filled with you (returning), you will begin to realize that you are changing. You will begin to feel unrestricted and even unable to be quite as frightened as you have been in the past. You will find that part of you does not seem to frighten so easily and will not be motivated to action by fear as it once was. Part of you will not care one way or another if you are in a panic. This is the part of you who is being awakened and now knows that fear is leaving and is no longer necessary.

It is not that you are being programmed to not care what happens to you. It is more that you are being given options on how to create and you will no longer use fear to create. When you have reached this phase in your transformation you will begin to see how you can use whatever you like to motivate you. You, for the most part, have always used fear and often money as motivators. Sex is also very big with you as a motivator. In this new world that you are creating you will actually use joy and love as motivators. It will be a short time before this catches on, but, once it does, it will be very popular.

As you begin to move from one way of creating into another way of creating, you will also begin to shift how you perceive your creations. Perception will allow you to be in a different position in order to receive what you are now creating. In the past you may have been stuck in a certain perception that caused you to miss your created good when it came. It's sort of like missing the train, or not being home when a delivery arrives. You may not connect with your own creation if your perspective is a little off or even "way off." You may have been creating great things all your life but just missing them as they arrived. You may now learn to know when your good is coming and be in position to receive it. You will find that you no longer require so much pain and punishment in your life when you stop creating from fear. As you create more and more from joy you will be adding to your joy, just as creating from fear has added to your fear. You are in a position now to receive and to love you. In receiving and loving you, you begin to receive and love "all of you" and creation is "all of you."

When you first begin to take on light you will feel elated, and you will begin to see how you are no longer being a frightened person. You will begin to feel as though everything in your life is okay and you are not even concerned about tomorrow or what the future holds. This is a point at which you may feel as though you have slipped into complacency and tedium. This, of course, is not how you were programmed to behave and so you will not be comfortable with self-satisfaction and boredom. You are accustomed to living on the verge of panic and trouble and pain and discomfort. If you feel comfort for too long you get bored. You get worried that you might sleep too much or rest too much or be lazy.

Most of you do not know how to relax. You think that relaxing is going out and celebrating, or going to a carnival, or going out dancing, or to a party. This is not relaxing. Relaxing is reposing in a state of calm and peace. You believe that mowing your lawn or puttering in your flower bed is relaxing because it requires no mental stress. When you really relax you lie down and focus on your body and allow your muscles to unwind and relax – hence the word, relax! How can you relax if your muscles are on the go and you are moving all over the place? This is not relaxing, it is energy moving and it results in a zing effect and the end result is you all over the place.

The point I am trying to make is to stop zinging all the time. Get in your zing time but also get in your rest and relaxation. It is most important to allow you to rest in between your clearings. You are taking off huge loads of programming and you are beginning to unearth "you" who have been buried for a very long time. As you unearth you, you will find you are not all that well in certain ways and you will require great amounts of rest and relaxation. Do not worry when you must rest for a week and not go zinging off in all directions. This rest time will allow you to mend from this psychic surgery that is being done on you to remove all of your unnecessary baggage and programming.

As you begin to release old layers of "burden by guilt" you will begin to feel as though you have been hit by a truck on the freeway. Just rest and allow your body the time that it requires to heal. You will find that as you heal you will become very elated until the next truck comes and hits you. You will begin to see your pattern in clearing your past programming and your perception will oh-so-gradually begin to shift. As you see how you are at last beginning to see the light, you will wish to know that you have taken part in the birth of God in man. You have gone through your own pain in order to walk out of your pain and leave it behind. As you begin to leave behind your pain you will feel lost and a loss. You have never lived without pain and it has been with you for a very long time! When you begin to live without pain you will have crossed over into joy and freedom from guilt. You will have walked through the valley of darkness and come through without a scratch on you (well, except for that truck on the freeway that hit you several times).

When you begin to know that you are on your way out of the valley of darkness you will feel a bit lost. Your whole life will have changed because you will have changed. Once you walk out into the light, you will feel that you need to re-collect your old programming in order to get you motivated. You will try on fear but fear will no longer play the role of motivator for you. Next you will try guilt or pain to motivate you and nothing will work. You must now find a new motivator and this one will be love. Out of love of self you will begin to care for and nurture your own self. No more trying to give you away to another to be fed, be it spiritually or mentally or emotionally. You will become your own divine caregiver and you will no longer feel like part of you is missing. You will be totally whole and contained "in" you. You will love you enough to want to keep you and you will care for you as you would a precious child. You will be loved and nurtured and you will be held in very high esteem by you, for you will know the value and the greatness of you. You will not fall down in your esteem, for you have spent far too many lifetimes in low self-esteem and that is in the past for you.

As you begin to walk into your future you will carry your head high and you will know that you are God and you are the creator as well as the creation, and you will not be shamed nor will you find fault. You will have turned a corner, and this corner will have led you to the truth and the truth will have set you free. The truth is that you cannot be bad because there is no bad. You can only be good and you can only be God. There is no one else for you to be. Evil does not exist and you are no part of it. What does that leave you? You are left with God. You have no one to believe in but God, and you are God.

So, I suggest that you begin to accept your new role. You have played the devil long enough. Now it is time to play God. You got to see how it feels to be bad and now you will see how it feels to be good. You have felt bad and now you are going to feel good. It is all coming to you. It is just around the corner. You are peeling away the bad so that the good may shine through. You are beginning to change and to grow in a new direction. I am sorry for any pain and inconvenience you may suffer in this great time of change and healing. It is all part of the process and it will soon pass as will all pain and suffering. You are on a path to peace and it is paved in gold. You will reach out and touch God and, in doing so, you will see how you came to be.

*A*s you begin to overcome your own fears you will find that you no longer regard fear as you once did. You will no longer see fear as such a negative aspect in your life, as you will no longer be living in constant fear and self put-down. When you live in constant fear you begin to know only fear. Constant fear can be a state of mind and it may be alive in the subconscious.

When you have constant fear it will manifest in various areas of your life. Say you are a victim in this life, and this victim role is one of being or having been incested by a parent or relative. If you have blocked the incident out of your conscious mind in order to preserve your sanity, you will find that you lived in the fear state. If you are now healing, you will allow this fear to come to the surface so that you might experience it and release it. It is not so dangerous now that you are older and have a more evolved perspective. You will begin to release your fear and your emotions will begin to heal. As your fear is released it is siphoned into areas that it came through. These areas are usually areas that once flowed with trust and happiness. As your fear became encrusted throughout the years, your trust and happiness became mistrust and sorrow. Hence we have a mistrusting person who cannot find happiness.

When you begin to release the fear that is blocking your trust and happiness you become a little confused. You now want to trust but are not sure how to, and you want happiness but expect pain to be attached to it. Your joy as a child was attached to pain if you are playing a victim. So, as you begin to release the fear that is blocking trust and happiness, you will begin to feel some struggle between the old way and the new way. As you grow through this you will begin to feel more and more trust and happiness. After all, trust and happiness are what being God is all about. Trust and happiness are yours by the simple fact that you enter into them when you enter creation.

As you begin to see more trust and happiness enter your life, you will begin to see love light up places within you that you did not know you had. You will begin to feel as though you were being born new and free for the very first time. You will feel like a teenager who is just discovering life for the very first time. When you see all life through the eyes of trust you will automatically begin to see happiness. You will begin to know that you are not only well on your way to rising above the old world of pain and sorrow and mistrust, you are also on your way up even higher in this ascension process. As you move higher and higher you will have greater clarity about the "game of life," and you will remove yourself from the pain and the burden of forcing yourself to play blindfolded. You will have come out of the dark and you will be literally living in the light.

When you begin to live in the light you will be reconnecting to your source. Light is your source and light is all that really is. When you reconnect you will become even more elated than you thought you could be, for you will then be part of everything and everything will flow to you. You may spend years trying to learn ways to out maneuver your blocks to the flow (your fears) in order to create good for yourself, or you can simply bring your blocks to the surface and deal with them. When your blocks are gone you are free to give and to receive. When you force yourself to give or to receive and your blocks (fears) are in place, you create more energy blocks by pushing against the old ones. I highly suggest that you wait and use your time and energy to "raise" your blocks. In doing so, you will be raising you. You may try to create and manifest and draw all good to you, but you will block it or destroy it if you have fear in those areas.

Do not push you to create more stuff. Instead, assist you in the rise up to allow everything in. Once you have raised the dense parts of you, you will be free to give and receive in a steady flow; no barricades to block anything. Your walls and dams will have come down. Actually, they will have gone "up" to a higher level of consciousness to be received and released. Everything must be received or admitted in order to be released. Denial blocks you up and admittance, or admitting to, allows you to enter it and receive it and own it and do something about it. If you only deny parts of you or situations in you, you are pushing you further away and you are creating walls and dams and blocks. Do not block your flow with the source. Do not back you up more than you already are. It is time to move forward and it is time to allow God to show you your fears. I know you do not want to look at your fears but it will set you free and it will make you whole.

Whenever you feel like you do not wish to be in pain and whenever you feel like your life is a mess, I wish you to remember that you are creating something out of nothing. When you are creating something out of nothing, you cannot see what you are creating until it crosses that line from nothing to something.

As you learn to treat yourself with love and respect, you will be learning love and respect. As you learn to create life with love and respect, you will be projecting out love and respect. As you project out love and respect, you will draw more love and respect to you. Are you upset that you do not receive love and respect? It is not necessary to get upset about it. Simply begin to treat yourself in the manner you wish to be treated. If you wish to have kindness in your life then I suggest that you begin to treat you with kindness. If you wish to have love in your life then I suggest you begin to treat you lovingly. You will find that "what you are" is what you project, and what you project is what you get right back. This is not punishment; it is simply a way to show you what you are projecting.

When you begin to clear out your subconscious programming, you will find that you will be creating more of you to fill the void where the programming was stored. You may fill this void with self-love and this will begin to gain and take over momentum, and soon self-love will be bigger than self-hate and self-loathing. When self-love grows to the extent that you are bigger in love than you are in hate, you will see a big change in how others react to you. Now you are projecting love of self and it is being reflected back to you.

You have never been taught to love you. You were born into this world and told from early on that you must learn to love and care for your brothers and sisters. Some were told to love and care for their parents and cousins and aunts and uncles and grandparents, and the pet dog and pony and squirrels in the yard. No one ever took you aside and said "the most important thing you will ever do is to love and care for yourself." You just were not taught to love you. It is not accepted and I wish to change how you believe. I want you to accept you (all aspects of you) and to love you. Love you as you would love a most valued family member, or, for some of you, the way you would love a most valued pet or possession.

You are learning to accept you by uncovering what you hide. What you hide is usually what you hate about yourself and it is usually a perspective you have adopted from early in childhood. You are learning to allow these perceptions to change and to transform. If you were repeatedly told how you were stupid or ugly or both, you will begin to see how you fell into agreement with that, and how you created a place to hide that part of yourself from the one (or ones) who called you by these names. As you grew you carried these hidden parts of you and now we are taking them out to look at them and release them. So, how will you know when you are looking at them and letting them go? Simple; if the programming was ugly and stupid, you will begin to feel ugly and stupid as they rise up in you. When they have gone, you wonder how you could have ever believed yourself to be ugly and stupid.

Now; the interesting thing is how you have just changed a projection. You are now projecting "I am beautiful (or handsome) and I am intelligent." You will now draw like. Like attracts like. If you hate yourself you will draw others who hate themselves. Because they hate themselves they find fault everywhere so, of course, they will have no problem finding fault within you, because you also hate yourself and are trying to hide your ugliness and stupidity. Now that you have taken that hidden aspect, or perspective, and looked at it you have released it. Now you are drawing those who reinforce your new perspective which is "I love me for I am God."

You will find that like attracts like and soon you will have many in your life who not only see themselves as beautiful, but see you as beautiful also. This is how creation works. You can change your perspective by allowing yourself (all parts of yourself) to be seen and heard. You may communicate with all levels of your beingness without judgment and without criticism. When you have learned to do this, you will know that criticism and judgment are no longer necessary, and so you will let them go and receive love and acceptance to fill that empty space. Every time you "clear" out part of you, you automatically replace that part with something else. You usually replace that part of you with what you are currently learning or teaching yourself to believe. Since you are reading this material, you have been programmed for self-love and self-acceptance.

This is the purpose of this series of "God speaks" information. You wanted help. You asked for a better way. I sent out a volunteer who is willing to spend the time working on herself in order to get this information to you. She did and is doing her job well. She is one of you and you are like her. You will find that she has often suffered in her own clearing process, and she does not claim to know more than you. She simply gave up and allowed God to use her body to the extent that was necessary to bring this information to you. You will find that "creating" works in many ways and it is manifested in many forms. I know that you all want riches but you also want joy. Your need for riches stems from your need for joy. If you were totally joyful you would not care about money. Yet you all want money because it will bring you peace of mind which will bring joy. You are tired of struggling so you want money so you do not need to struggle. Your only misconception is that money does not bring an end to struggle.

The enemy to joy is within you. You are beginning to see how you are layered and constructed, and you are beginning to know that your joy has been cut off by part of you. You will find that you no longer require struggle when you begin to allow yourself to love you. You will find that when you "clear" your belief and self-loathing and self-hatred, you will be allowing an opening for self-love and self-joy. You will begin to feel joy once you begin to feel self-love. The world may crumble and fall around you but you will not care. Your joy will keep you warm and happy. You will not be an idiot out in a storm screaming and laughing. You will be truly centered in joy, and conflicts outside of you will have no more effect on you than watching a movie. You will be centered in your own self-love and fear will have gone.

As you begin to allow yourself to become all knowing, you will find that you are not so critical of how you respond in certain situations. You will find that as you begin to realize that all response is simply a matter of choice, you will begin to see how you need not adhere to certain rules and regulations governing appropriate and inappropriate behavior. You will find that you are no longer in the field of battle between right and wrong. You will have turned in your struggle against yourself for peace and love of self.

As you learn to release your hold on old judgments that you have held against yourself, you will find that you will be freeing up more of you and allowing yourself to become more of you. In the world as you know it, you often close down parts of you in order to shut them down or off. You began this from birth as you are trained to not do this or not do that. As you shut more and more of you off, *you* begin to be less and less. You have been shutting down until eventually there isn't much left and so you die. You are now opening up and becoming more of you by lifting the restrictions or limits that you have previously placed on you.

You are about to discover what it feels like to be whole. You have always been complete, but you did not use all of you. You did not know that you could or you did not think it to be a good idea. Now you are learning to deal with all of these lost or hidden aspects of yourself, and you may embrace them and begin to use them in more positive ways. All parts of you have a good use, even anger and rage. All parts of you are acceptable and all parts of you are also part of God. You are everything and everything is you.

When you begin to become more of you, you will be put in a position to integrate all of your new found feelings and wisdom. This process of integration may take some time as you still live in a world where you use time. As this integration process takes place you will be allowed to feel some of your emotions and to know that you are in touch with them. You will then be allowed to replace any unnecessary emotion and to receive all that is allowable in the way of changed feelings. In the same way that you change your mind you may change your feelings. You may do this at any given moment.

So, when your feelings begin to run away with you, you might simply change to a different feeling. If you are unable to change the feeling and it seems to be overpowering you, then I suggest you go with it and allow it to surface and release. If it is a powerful enough feeling you can release it by screaming (in your car away from others) or crying (in private please) or hitting your bed or pillow. Stomping is also good to release powerful emotions. Outside is best for this one.

Once you have assisted the emotion in its release and it has less power over you, try to simply change the feeling into something else. This is possible and you will have cleared the most powerful part of your original feeling, so that it will not have the built up energy required to push down the preferred feeling that you now wish to express. Everything is a choice, even how you feel. If the feelings are too strong for you, simply run with them until you can easily change to a new feeling. This is getting what you want, by allowing the emotional data banks within to release their charge and get their energy out. When you have eventually released all charge, you will not even find it necessary to stop and think about what you feel or why you feel a certain way.

As you become more and more clear of old charge and programming, you will be allowed to see how you are not only 'not' your programming, you are actually above your programming and not even a part of it. For now you *feel* like it is all you and what you are. You even say, "This is just the way I am." But you are not. Not the real you anyway. So; as you begin to release and to clear the old feelings, you will experience these feelings, and gradually, when you have released enough of the charge behind the feeling, the feeling will then fizzle and you can insert whatever feeling you want. You may then ask for and receive "joy." Do not bother to ask for power for you are coming out of that phase of creation. You have the power and look how you have used it – without joy!

*

You are now at a time of great change which, of course, will cause great concern and annoyance and disturbance and confusion. It will be a time of change within, which will be reflected out and it will be seen everywhere you look. For most of you it will be a time of healing and growth. With healing and growth you begin to see how you are not only no longer sick, you are also no longer willing to be sick. You will heal and you will relish your wellness. As you begin to see how good wellness can feel you will wish to remain well and happy. For when you are in wellness you are in your whole state. Wholeness is a connectedness between your body, mind and spirit. Wholeness is a wellness that runs through all three and allows all three to be complete in their very connection. When you become whole you will no longer be fragmented and scattered. When you release your hold on fear you will be in your right state which is whole/complete/oneness.

When you have reached this state of entirety you will no longer feel lost/separated/divided. You will be united in yourself and this will create a feeling (inside) of complete calm and peace. The struggle within will have ended and you will have begun to transform what was once separation into "one." You will have sent your own creation out to create wholeness for you by participating in the creation of the one creating. You will literally be the creator and the creation re-creating what the creator is. You will have transformed what you were, into what you are. You will have consciously taken part in re-creating you so that more of you might "be." You will have knowingly made you into more of you. This is the creator at work. You will be taking responsibility for creating more of you. You create you. You always have. You have convinced yourself that someone outside of you creates you, but it is all you! You are the creator and you are the creation.

Now; you are much larger than what you currently believe, so don't get all frightened and begin to think what a mess you are. This portion of you that you are "aware" of is but a small portion, and you are simply a pinpoint in this part of you. You are actually so big that human consciousness does not have the capacity to take in the totality of you. You are grand indeed. You stretch everywhere and you do not end. There are so many of "you" that you could never count them all, but you actually have no need to. It would be pointless, like counting the grains of sand on a beach. It has no value.

So as you begin to change and to realize your potential for growth you will be allowed to move into greater parts of you. By "you" I mean your consciousness. You (your consciousness) will learn to shift its position and take on a new point of view with relative ease. This will allow you to be in many positions simultaneously and, therefore, to expand the conscious self as well as the unconscious self. So, as you begin to shift from one position or stance to another remember to keep it moving. You are growing now so don't stop the growth. You are shifting-up now so don't stop midway and settle in. It is not a complete shift until you feel the thrust forward and then it will be smooth riding, or sailing, for you. As you learn to expand your consciousness more and more, you will learn to see how you are also expanding what you are. What you are is the totality of everything, and in expanding your consciousness you are making room for you to accept all parts of you. As you begin to accept these parts your consciousness will stretch even further to accommodate new growth/wisdom/insight.

So... you are growing. You are a seed that was planted and is now sprouting and taking off. A seed can be as little or as big as any "idea." When an idea is planted it begins to grow and to expand. Now that idea is in its first stages of growth and you will feel it as change. Hold on and don't be afraid. You are on a ride that will take you up. How high up? Well – you decide. You can grow tall or you can stop short. The choice is yours and it's really not important which decision you make. You are learning about you and it is all you, so the part that stops short is just the same as the part that goes on. It is all you. You are traveling and experimenting and creating. Who says a tall building is better than a short building. You decide what you want and then create out of your own conscious choice. This is how it was meant to be. No judgment! Only choices.

You will begin to see how you do not wish to be in anger and pain. You only wish to be in joy and love. As your pain subsides you will be allowed to feel how you are not only good, you are also loving. You are a loving being and you only express what you have been taught to express. You express your anger because anger was most often used when training you. This is from past life as well as from this life. Anger was and is a big part of any training process. I believe the statement from your Bible is "Spare the rod and you will spoil the child." Anger has been used between couples in the same manner. You get angry and then you get even. When, or after, you get even you feel better. Some of you feel better after you scream at another and some of you feel better after a good fight. You are all releasing anger and you are all becoming more loving by doing so. You may continue to use your anger to get up your courage, but I suggest that you simply show courage in any given situation and pass the anger over. You will learn to hold your screaming without it becoming explosive within you. You will learn to come into balance in all parts of you.

As you learn to become more and more balanced you will be becoming more and more calm. When you are calm you are not so upsetable and your anger will not be so out of control. You know when you are angry but you do not always admit that you are. Some of you try to ignore your anger and this will only push it down deeper within you. As you learn to be totally "in" you, you will learn that all unwanted behaviors will automatically come to the surface and be released.

Be thankful when you have an opportunity to see your feelings in any given situation. This allows you to change your feelings. If you do not change your feelings you will continue to feel the way you have always felt which is, for the most part, very unlovable. I do believe it is time to be lovable and to allow yourself to be loved by you. When you love you, you have no anger at you and you will no longer feel the need to get back at you. Your self-destructive ways will end and you will not be in so much pain. Your pain will begin to ease when you can truly accept that you are okay. When you know that you are lovable you will accept gifts freely without fear that you must return tit-for-tat. This old karmic cycle will die and you will be left with only "receiving everything" instead of the old belief or pattern which is "you only get back what you put out."

You are learning to be your own creator as well as your own creation. In this way you constantly receive and you constantly give off. It is simply the flow of everything that is. It is how you live and do not realize that you do. Life is a flow. Sure, it has its ups and downs and even a few blocks here and there, but you will soon learn to flow into your own life without the daily struggle. Struggle will end when you have been good enough to you. Struggle will end when you have taken care of your feelings. Struggle will end when you can be you without fear of what anyone will say, do, or think of you. You will "know" that you are lovable and "in the knowing" you will receive love from the source of love which is God. You turn your love "off" or "on" by your acceptance or rejection of it.

When you begin to see how you are programmed to fear, you will begin to see how separation occurs. Fear sets in and you begin to suspect and become wary of those who are not like you in certain ways. In actuality you are like everyone as you are "all one." With your perception of separation comes your perception of evil or bad. You do not like what you do not understand. You cannot relate to what you do not like and you are very likely to push it away if you do not like it. As you get to see more and more of what you are by reacting with others, you will get to see how you react within your own self. You are both sides of everything and you are being put in a position to face the side of you that you have distaste for. When you have seen how you have distaste for yourself, you will be given the opportunity to let go of that judgment and to change it if you do not like it. "It" being the essence in you that you find distasteful. It may be that you decide to find it okay and you decide to keep this essence after all. Maybe it has enhanced your life, or maybe it was just necessary for a short time and now it is no longer necessary.

When you begin to look into you, you will discover that you are basically having a rough time with your *perception* of what is actually going on. You believe that what you see is what is occurring when, in actuality, what you see is simply what you choose to see. You learn to see and hear things that do not exist and you do this to protect yourself because of past hurt or pain. It is not necessary to feel pain, and it is not necessary to continue to view your world through the old pain that is programmed into you. As you begin to view your reality through joy, you will see it as totally joyous no matter what occurs. You simply will not have the ability to "look for" any pain. You will feel good, because your outlook will be that of joy. You need not focus on pain, and you need not mistrust your eyes because you think you see one thing and, in actuality, you are looking at something else. You are not seeing wrong, you are simply looking through tinted or tainted glasses. Your eyes see only what you will allow them to see and you are being programmed by what you "believe" that you see. This too is changing and you will begin to see the good in all things soon.

As you begin to readjust your view of your entire perception of life, you will begin to go in and out of focus. You will see it one way one moment and see it another the next moment. This is, of course, due to the use of your new perceptions and the blending of old perceptions. When you move totally into the new, you will be part of your own joy. You will see it and be in it. You will become so much a part of your joy that you will wish to be free to float and fly. You will feel so light that you will truly feel as though a giant weight has been lifted. That weight will be pain. You will walk away from pain and begin the shift "up" into joy. Now remember, whenever you shift up it takes a few moments to adjust and to begin to move at a smoother momentum. Allow yourself time to see what you are seeing and to change it to what is real. Joy is real; pain is the illusion that has been created. It is false.

When you begin to raise your level of awareness and to shift into this new reality of joy, you will find parts of you wish to stay behind in the pain, for they are comfortable with what they have always known. As you teach yourself to allow joy by "receiving" joy, you will be teaching yourself to allow your pain to leave. Pain is not a part of you. It was made to do a job and it is no longer necessary. Most of what you use pain for is no longer necessary. You may get the same effect from joy as you now receive from pain. You will find that as you change from one to the other, you will be "between" and a little confused by both. Hang on to hope and hope will carry you through to your other side. You are literally going from one side of you to the next. You are going from pain into joy. You are moving through you and seeing this reflected in your world. You are looking at you and projecting what you see onto the world. Stop projecting what you think you see and begin to project what you really are.

When you begin to see how you are transforming, you will begin to know more about your own past. As you move into your new identity you are allowed to see your old identity as it leaves you. You will be able to see old patterns and old beliefs and you will experience old hurts and old annoyances. As these things begin to leave you, you will find that you are no longer attached to holding on to them and you are no longer attached to being a certain way.

When you learn that everything is only a choice, you will begin to allow yourself to make choices without condemning yourself for any given choice. You will also be allowing your neighbors to make choices without condemning them for their choices. This will be a very big step for you, as you have always made choices and then judged these choices. Usually you prejudge so that when things fall through you can say, "See, I told you so." This allows you to be right which helps you to feel like you have "value" and are "smart" and "good." This is a technique that you have been using to build yourself so that you feel strong and mighty and good. You are so tired of feeling stupid and vulnerable and wrong. All of these emotions are attached to pain of rejection and fear of loss. You have been programmed to "achieve" and so you "compete" with one another on a daily basis. You outdo this one or that one, and you begin to feel as though your only source of glory is to be the one who does the best work, or is the smartest, or makes the best grades (only now you use money instead of grades).

So, as you begin to grow and to transform, you will be learning to not judge where you are. If you can flow with your life and know that everything is in perfect order, you will know that you are healing and becoming God. God does not birth in ways that you would expect. God comes in and cleans things out and makes changes. God does not arrive and offer you more pain. God does, however, clean out your storerooms of existing pain and this cleaning process may take some time. After all, how long did it take to receive all the pain you carry? How many lifetimes of pain and judgment are heaped on a pile inside of you? How do you expect to release all of your pain and not feel any of it go? It is not that it would be an impossibility, but you are not that evolved at this time. So, I must work within you from where you are.

You are beginning to see how you are full of hurt and anger and physical pain as well as emotional pain. You are being cleaned out, and you are releasing all that is outdated and no longer conducive to your spiritual/mental/physical body. You are replacing fear with love and this will create understanding. One of the things you will begin to understand is your judgment and how it may or may not serve you. Do not beat yourself up for not being this way or that way. You are being changed; transformed. How do you know how you should or should not be? Allow yourself to begin to experience new ways of being, and you will be allowing yourself greater expansion and a whole new attitude towards your own existence.

Once you begin to see how many possibilities await you, you will be amazed. Right now the majority of you believe that big bucks will bring big happiness. I want to show you how many ways it is possible to bring joy and happiness; not just one way but billions of ways. You will begin to discover new parts of you and these new parts each carry new pieces to your puzzle. As you uncover more and more of you, you will begin to realize that there is so much you have not yet taught yourself and there is so much you have not yet allowed yourself to receive. You will find that as you begin to give up parts of you that no longer serve you, you will be letting go and receiving at the same time. Letting go allows you to make room for more of you (God) to come in.

You will find that you are not only 'not' being all that you could be, you are not even a fraction of your potential. You want power, you want riches? I suggest you begin to allow all of you to come into you and then you will see creation at its best. Right now you are just playing at creation with a pinpoint of light. When you are creating with a giant beam you will see some pretty big changes in your life and in your world. You are no more than a grain of sand at this moment. You are, however, turning into the entire beach just by waking up to who and what you are.

When you finally discover how big you are, then you can "consciously" decide what you need and what you don't need. For now, your consciousness is so small that you are like a tiny baby who screams when he drops his toy. He does not know what is really going on, he only feels the loss of his toy. You can feed a baby but he will spit it out because he does not know he must eat to live. I am spoon feeding you now and you sometimes spit out as much as I have put in you. You are being deprogrammed and you are spewing misinformation at others and for yourself. Stay calm and allow God to spoon feed you and do not try to figure out how right or wrong your life is.

When you begin to see how forgiveness is all about your own judgments you will begin to see how you are judging and condemning you to pain and suffering. Each time that you get so involved as to judge another and want revenge on another, you begin to tear at the fiber of you. You are made to feel your emotions and you are the one who is most directly affected by them. If you could just learn to not react or respond by revenge you would be saving yourself a great deal of pain. You can tell how much revenge you carry by how you wish pain or sorrow or harm for others. In some cases you are the only one that you believe deserves punishment, so you will only see your level of revenge based on how severe you believe you must be with you. If you treat you with fairness and appreciation you will no longer feel the need to make you pay or suffer for past sins. Everything on this planet is based on the "justice" system and I would like you to rise above justice and be loving. You cannot be loving and be punishing. It does not work. If you love you, you do not feel it necessary to punish you. I will show you an example:

Once upon a time I allowed parts of me to enter matter. These parts became so confused after separating from me that they began to take on a personality of their own. Each personality was different and yet it was the same. The major personality trait was fear and the major fear was that of being hurt in some way. As pain began to grow, this major personality trait of fear began to fear its own creation. Fear had created pain and now pain was taking over fear. As fear began to contemplate how to regain control, he began to realize that the best way to stop pain is to end fear. He decided to end and to change to another form of energy in order to continue. Fear changed into love and now judgment has no place. Pain is now confused and does not know his right place so he is popping up everywhere. As pain begins to fizzle (as he cannot survive without fear to lead him) he will change to something else also. For this to take place we must let go of our need for pain. As long as you believe in justice you must have a way to promote your justice. Pain is a good way to get people to listen. Put the fear of God into them and if that does not work put the fear of pain into them.

You have all been overloaded with this justice system. Everything from stealing apples off God's trees to child abuse, and even yelling at the dog, must all change. You must begin to see everything differently than you have been taught. Pretend you were born thousands of years from now and there is no justice because each individual has let go of pain. There will be no crime and there will be no feeling of guilt and separation from love, because you "all" will have returned to love. When you have love it permeates everything and it spills over and takes over to the extent that nothing is seen as evil.

You will love being in love. You will enjoy your feelings as never before and you will know that you have been touched by God and that God is touching you. You will know that you have reached out to the purest form and touched God on the shoulder, and God did not shrink back from you nor did he wish to punish you. God will look you full in the face and love and accept you unconditionally, and this is how you will be treated and it is how you will treat others. Once judgment goes there will be bliss. No one is telling you to stop this instant and change. You are so programmed to go forward into pain that were you to stop now and turn around, it would be like trying to stop a giant freight train with sixty boxcars behind it. You can only work from where you are. For now, you are in pain and I am simply pointing to a direction that will allow your pain to change into something a little more healing and a little less destructive.

As you sit and read and learn, you are actually beginning the process by which you might change and grow. You are so cluttered and bogged down by old programming that you (most of you) believe it's a good idea to take a life for a life. Those of you who believe the opposite, that no one has the right to take a life, are just as confused. It will be in the center that you find your balance. As you learn to walk the center line you will see how far left of the truth and how far right of the truth you have come. Be at peace and know that in your future you will not care if justice exists and you will not care who dies. You will have come to understand and appreciate creation, which is you.

When you begin to see the difference between loving you and not loving you, you will begin to see how to change bad feelings toward yourself into good feelings towards yourself. You are learning to love you and this does not mean that you kick you around verbally or emotionally. When you love you, you allow you to be your own best friend and you no longer allow you to be your own worst enemy. When you begin to see how others are only treating you the way "you" are treating you, you will begin to change how you treat you. You will begin to find joy in being you and you will begin to find yourself quite nice to be with. At some point you will learn to know you and to love you without asking much of you. You will learn to know your own true identity and to know how to be the best friend you ever had.

When you learn to be your own best friend, you will also learn to be the one who cares about you enough to take real good care of you. You will no longer depend on others for your emotional well-being and you will no longer depend on others for your happiness. You will have learned that you are your own creator and you will therefore create whatever is best for you (your best friend). When you learn to create only the best for you it will come from you and to you. You now create from you and to you but you do not realize how you do this. You are not even sure how you are here let alone how you create more of what you get.

For the most part, you will begin to realize how you are no longer being put in the position of creator when you turn that position over to God. You will find that even though you are God you are also human, and the human part of you will do best to rest and to heal. As you allow the spirit part of you to take control of your life, you may see change and you may not like all that you see. Spirit is quite convinced that you do not require all that you (ego/human-self) believe that you require to make you happy and keep you well. He (Spirit) may decide to take hold of your life and create some positive growth that will feel awful to you if you are *stuck* firmly in the material world. This human condition is one of being petrified in fear-based energy. You have literally turned to stone in certain areas of your belief in what "you must have or you will die." When you learn to come out of these beliefs of "all or none," you will be allowing you to move back into the flow. Your solid belief of necessity will begin to crumble and will be replaced by a new belief that carries a new perspective.

You are all changing and you are all learning new ways to live that you have never before experienced. Each of you will begin to experience what you most need to get you *unstuck*. If this is unpleasant for you please remember the story I told you regarding the dog who is all wrapped up in barbed wire and screeching for help. God is unwrapping this wire that has held you prisoner, and once you get all the barbs out of you, you will be free and you will no longer feel restricted, nor will you feel the pain of the wire that has bound you and cut into your skin for so long. You must be patient as God does his work and unravels what you have gotten yourself caught up in. Do not get up and run off half-cocked, or half-unwound, and begin spouting off about how you are free and you know how to get free. Stay calm. Allow God to show you the way. I know you are impatient and in a state of unrest. You will receive all that is meant for you and you will also receive God.

When you begin to see how good it feels to have your binding removed you may get a little cocky and begin to show off. Try to stay calm and try to be as pleasant to the others, who are still having their bindings removed, as possible. You need not show off how intelligent you are or how free you are. Walk softly and show kindness to others. Do not be afraid to assist if you are asked. God will guide you to where you are needed. Do not be afraid to be your own best friend and to discuss your own good fortune with yourself. I know that you are taught to not speak to yourself and it is thought to be a form of craziness, but I would like you to talk with you and listen to you and learn about you. Say it or write it and let you answer your own questions. How else can you get to know you if you are never allowed to talk with you? Can you imagine living your entire life next door to someone and never once saying "hello?" This is what you do.

No one ever told you to get to know you by talking and asking questions. You only know how to put you down when you do wrong. You don't even know how to give yourself gifts. You think that if you are good you deserve a big night out or a new car. You don't know about true nurturing of your body, your psyche, your mind. You will learn a great deal about you by talking with you and learning more about how you really feel about things. After all, you are the one who has been creating for you all of your life. Don't you want to find out why you created what you did and how you can change what you no longer wish to create?

You will learn that the more you get to know you the better friends you will become with you. You are going to live with you for the rest of your life. The least you can do is talk with you and get to know you. You may find that you actually enjoy your own company and you may also find that you are a pretty nice person. You may have some surprises as to what you really feel about certain issues but, for the most part, you will be most appreciative for this opportunity to get to know you!

As you begin to move through your own created reality, you will begin to view more of what you want and to let go of those ideas that no longer work for you. As you learn to see how you are behaving, you will wish to change your pattern of behavior or to let go of your old programming in favor of new, evolved thought.

As you release old ideas, you will begin to see how you were the one who was holding you back and you will begin to let go of blame. Blame is creating shame, and shame of course adds to guilt. If you want to be at peace and to let go of pain you must release your hold on blame. Blame will keep you locked in to a good guy vs. bad guy mentality. When you believe in good vs. evil, you must punish one and reward another. Usually good is rewarded but not always. You may find that you have mixed emotions or feelings about what is good and what is bad. You may begin to see how you have created your own set of rules based on what you were taught in the past. As you begin to release your hold on the need to be "right," you will be letting go of the need to see things one way.

When everything is said and done, there are as many ways as there are entities on this plane. When you begin to know how you have created from either black (wrong) or white (right), you will begin to know how you have shut out light by making certain choices black, when in actuality everything is light to one degree or another. When you can learn to allow everything to be, you will be very flexible indeed. So far you are stretching and growing quite well, and soon you will be so flexible that you will be allowed to expand beyond your current limited thought.

As you expand more and more, you will be growing in love and you will be working within your own creative thought system to produce a greater thought system. You are being led into other areas simply by your willingness to expand and to grow beyond your current limited thought. Limited thought is choking you and cutting you off from the flow. Limited thought is bringing you to the surface of your own wasted life. Limited thought is pushing you right out of you. With limited thought you cannot expand, you can only contract. Unlimited thought allows you to expand and become bigger. This is what you want, but you have never known how to expand other than spreading out your wealth and your power. What you were really looking for was spiritual expansion which is now available to you.

So; as you expand you make more room or space for more unlimited thought. As you make more room or space you will be filled up with "source." The source flows in and takes over when there is space available. When space is provided for the source to move through you, you will begin to fill with greater amounts of creative source. As this source is allowed to move into you, you are transformed and begin to flow as the source flows. You and source become one. You and source begin to merge.

As you merge with source you begin to see as source sees. There is no wrong and everything becomes possible. This merging of you and source takes a little time and a little stretching on your part. You are being stretched now and you feel it. You may each experience this stretching in different ways depending on how limited or how constricted you have become. As you "loosen up" or "let go" or "chill out" you will be allowed to freely flow. You cannot freely flow when your beliefs are tied up in knots and your emotions are frozen in place. You will "chill out" by thawing out your frozen emotions. When you thaw out you will melt and warm up to the idea that you are indeed God. As long as you are blocked up and constricted and limited you will continue to believe that you are limited and bad and wrong. Now is the time to allow yourself to open up to new thought which will allow space for source to enter you. You could use a little more God source "in you."

As you begin to fill up you with more of you, you will realize how you never fully lived in you. You never really entered you and this is why your capacity for growth is so great. You have enormous potential and you have only used a small portion of what you are. You have the ability to be almost anything and you have the ability to perform great feats. As you learn more and more about your limitations you actually learn more about your way to freedom. By seeing how you have limited yourself you might see how to unlimit and expand. As you learn to expand, you will also be learning how to be all that you can be. When you begin to learn that you can be whatever you choose, you will no longer feel that you are trapped in certain situations. When you learn to let go of limitation, you feel "free" instead of restricted by life and the limitations you have placed on your life. When you begin to flow with the source, you will begin to see how you are not only no longer stuck in limitation, you are also no longer stuck in fear. Fear blocks you and restricts you, and you will begin to see this soon if you are not already seeing it.

When you begin to receive your new freedom you may wish to be "thankful," as thankfulness will keep you in a place of receiving. When you are thankful or grateful you create more of the same and, therefore, you have more to be grateful and thankful for. When you begin to see how you are getting freed up enough to "fly" you will want to take it easy. There will be a natural urge for you to relish your new-found freedom and to spread your wings and soar to new heights. Just remember that you still have the last effects of your programming and you may hit a block or two along the way. When this occurs do not be upset and do not lose hope. You have just begun to fly and you will not be soaring until you learn to glide.

As this process unfolds you will be feeling good, for your new-found awareness tells you that bad does not exist. You will be in a state of constant exhilaration as your new-found freedom from limitation will be so bountiful and so freeing. You will be elated and joyful to no longer be burdened by your fears and insecurities. When you reach this state your life will have a much less serious tone.

You will feel insecure as you will be in new territory, but, for the most part, you will be happy and free. Your life will begin to flow spontaneously and you will begin to flow within the source without blocking the source.

As this begins to occur you will see events begin to fall into place in your life. You will be living a life of ease and grace. You will also be flowing with love and peace. It will be a very good life and you are realistically close to it now. Your change in attitude and your shift in consciousness are your greatest assets. You have the ability to guide you into your own self to see what is blocking you from having it all. You may work yourself into a frenzy trying to create some good around your blocks or you can sit down, focus within and remove your blocks. This takes a little time but is well worth the effort.

You have seen a great deal in the time that you have read this series. It is often said that energy follows thought. I directed and guided you "in" to your own blocks. I pointed them out to you and said, "Look at what you do." This entire series of books was written to allow you to look within in an attempt to regain peace, love and God. You have looked within and some of you are still looking. You will learn to shift your focus as you go, and you will learn to see how you can change your entire reality by changing how you see reality. You have shifted and you have changed. You are now ready to see the light and to reach out and touch it. You are going to have a very bright future and it will be well worth being here for. You have no idea how great it is to be you and to walk with you into heaven. Heaven is next. You have walked the streets of hell and now you will walk the streets of heaven. It is your choice and it always has been. When enough of you scream for heaven and God, you get heaven and God.

You are now becoming more connected within your own electrical structure as well as your physical, mental and emotional bodies. When you have accomplished your first step up or shift up you will feel strange. You will not know quite what to do with yourself as you will now be at a new level, and this new level will not carry the rules that have always taken up so much space in your life. As you reach this new level you may not be comfortable at first. You may long for the past and the old ways. It is as though you have given up a drug and your body still craves the drug. In this case the drug was pain, be it physical or emotional pain it had the same effect on you. You will find that as you release pain your physical body will begin to rise to a new level of energy. It will have new strength and you will find yourself moving through life with greater ease. As you begin to see how you are becoming more fluid you will also see how you were stuck in the past, and this will allow you to make new, conscious choices. Do I want to continue this pattern or do I want to grow out of it?

As you make these conscious choices it is most gratifying to know that you are now in the driver's seat. At one time you were driven by pain and emotional anger or fear. Now it will become apparent to you that you are in charge of you, which gives you back ownership of you. This will dispel your old programming that tells you how you must do what is right or be unloved. Now you can do what is right for you and be loved by you. You lose no love and you are still self-accepted when you are taking responsibility for your own self. You are moving into an area now that will give you even greater responsibility. This is the area of godhood. As you "take on" God, you begin to see how you are moved into a specific position in order to receive God. In other words, if you were blocked you are opened up in specific areas so that you might begin to receive in just those areas. Once you begin to receive in the blocked areas, you will begin to know how you are changing. It will feel new and good to receive in areas that were previously blocked. You may walk around in wonder saying, "Gee, this is so unlike me. Wow, this feels good to do."

As you learn to take in more God force and unblock greater areas you will literally feel the shifts as they occur. You will feel like you were headed in one direction and all of a sudden you end up going in a totally different direction. This is sudden change and it is unnatural for most of you because you have all been taught to plan things out and then follow through. As you begin to see more and more sudden change in your life simply *accept it* please. It is okay to be spontaneous and it is okay to move in a new direction. You are spreading your wings here and learning to fly. So, as you begin to see how you are changing and growing into a whole new you, you will also see how you feel much better and your life moves instead of being stuck in the mud and debris of the past. This flow is what will keep you moving up and out of the clogged mire of your past. This shifting and changing and growing is you becoming all that you can be. It does not matter how old you are. You can begin to transform at any age and you can begin to change at any age.

When you begin to learn how you are a multi-dimensional being you will begin to be everywhere with all possibilities. Your limits are not cast in stone. You are evolving and changing, and as you do you are tearing down your walls of protection as well as your walls of fear. When you lock yourself behind walls, you live in a self-imposed prison. This is freedom time and you are breaking out and letting your walls fall to the ground. You will not require walls in your future. You will live in the moment and you will know that each choice that you make is a good choice, for it will lead you where you are going. All roads lead you to God. There is nowhere else to go.

When you begin to see how everything that you do is simply taught to you or learned by you, you will begin to see how you can re-teach yourself. You need never give up on you and simply allow the programming to take over. You are teachable and you want to learn. You are beginning to see how a limited belief system can create a limited life, and an expansive belief system can create a wide open, expansive life. You are in a process of being shown your limitations in order for you to expand upon them. The more flexible your belief system, the more flexible your life. If you wish to expand and grow out of limitation, I highly suggest that you spread out your beliefs and allow you to grow. It is up to you. Each individual controls his or her own belief system by controlling what he or she will allow in. If the fear of being fooled or tricked is great, they will put up walls of protection to guard against new hurt from new programming. The problem with most walls is that they block out everyone and everything, and you are left alone and lonely.

You are at a point in your development where you are willing to allow your walls to come down. This, of course, is in response to your quest for love. At this time your quest for love is very strong, and you do not want to block love by putting up walls. You are also not going to stop you by putting up walls. Walls are for keeping in things, and you want to let out a few unnecessary items. As you begin to release greater and greater quantities of pain, you will find that letting go of your walls of protection has actually let you out of your prison of pain. When the walls begin to come down you will begin to release your pain and your sorrow. You will begin to know peace of mind for the first time in a very long time. You will begin to feel as though you have a second chance at life, and you will begin to forgive yourself for holding on to so much garbage.

When your pain goes it will take with it the cause of your pain, which in most cases is a misunderstanding or a big judgment based in hurt. It could have been hurt feelings, or it could have been physical pain that was received at the hands of a loved one and never fully forgiven, nor was it well received. This, of course, is understandable. Who wants to receive pain? Well, actually, you do. You are addicted to it and you believe you deserve it and that is how it is drawn to you. You put out a signal that says "I need punishment because I was evil in a past life," and so you attract your punishment to you. You then get upset with those who do the deed and you refuse to forgive them. The next life rolls around and you hold a grudge, to the extent that you draw the same type of abuse just by holding the grudge against it. You are stuck in patterns and cycles, and I want you to let go of everything and just be. Do not judge it and do not hold on to it. By doing so, you create more of it.

When you begin to let down your barriers that have always protected you from more pain and sorrow, you will be allowing you out to see how to change your feelings regarding pain and sorrow. You will be allowing you to be put in a position to receive without judgment against how you receive. When you begin to trust again, you will begin to know that all that is good will come to you and you will know it as good. You will no longer fear 'bad.' You will no longer create 'bad.'

When you learn to let go of all that has been blocking you and holding you back, you will begin to see how you can flow with life and not block it or fight against the flow. It is a good thing to allow yourself to come out from behind your walls of protection. It is a good thing to know that you are taking good care of you, and it is a good thing to know that this transformation and healing process is a part of your life. You are changing and you are growing out of limitation. When you leave your prison do not be afraid of the freedom you now feel. Do not be afraid to spread your wings and fly. Do not be afraid to be free. You are meant to be free. It was never meant for you to be trapped and confined and restricted. Go for it! You are being set free now. You may fly or rest until you feel ready. You have come out of your own self-imposed prison of limitation, and you have unlimited your world by un-limiting your belief.

You will create your new world according to how you believe, with an option to change at any moment. This is flexibility and unlimited creation. You may continue to grow in thought, which will allow you to evolve to greater levels of growth and re-connectedness with the source. You are all coming back to God. You do not have to worry that you will not make it, for it is impossible to be anything but God.

You will begin to see how your electrical body carries information that affects your current life and how you react to life. You have been programmed to either defend yourself or to attack. This is on an elementary level and it has always been a part of you. Once you begin to lose your need to justify yourself you will lose your need to attack or defend. Most arguments and confrontations are a result of this type of behavior. When you begin to release your hold on fear of losing, you will no longer feel the need to defend or to attack. Some of you find yourself being afraid to do either, but you are feeling the urge. This is the control that was placed over you as a child and you want to break free and use your attack or defense strategies, but are so strongly programmed not to that you are stuck in your fear of doing the wrong thing. In such cases I would advise you to begin to see how you want to defend or attack, but do not act on it.

Be of a conscious mind as to how you are programmed, and begin to change your programming into something a little more useful. A good example would be to change to wisdom, which allows you to see how attack and defense are both the same energy going in opposite directions. When you have a strong need to defend yourself you are coming from attack energy. It is all the same line of energy. The best way to deal with a situation that is *perceived* as attack is to leave it. Walk away and don't engage the energy any further. You will learn to do this in the future and it will become very natural for you. You simply walk away like nothing happened. You don't walk away and criticize or nag about what happened, you just walk by like nothing happened. This disengages the energy that was coming at you and looking for a place to land.

Now; I do realize that certain situations are very hard for you to walk away from. This too will change in your future. You are changing; therefore, all that you create is changing also. When it comes to being in the front line of fire on a battlefield, I suggest you remember that you create all wars out of a need to be right and make others wrong. When you learn to let go of your need to be right you will also let go of your need to stand up and fight for yourself, your country, or your borders. Whatever you do you will do out of love, and fighting does not come out of love. Fighting comes out of hostility, and as long as you are hostile you will continue to find reasons to fight. It may look to you like you are simply defending yourself, but it will be fighting all the same.

The best way to deal with hostile energy is to release it in constructive ways. If you find that you constantly end up arguing or debating or trying to get your point across you are hostile. Get out your biggest pillow and beat up your bed before you start your day. This will release your pent-up emotions that you would normally release on others during your day. I am trying to get you to stop "acting out" on one another and begin to settle down and see peace.

You will begin to see how you are no longer being led around by your programming when you begin to change how you are programmed. Many of you will begin to see things in yourself that you do not want to keep, and you will begin to let go of these things. They may be desires or behavior patterns that are not necessarily healthy in nature. We are here to heal you and not to make you sick. You have been sick for a long time and now you are getting well. You have learned how to be so sick that you could no longer accept your current life. Now you will be well enough to not only accept your life, you will also accept you. No more rejection of you. From now on you are number one. You are number one concern and you are number one in your eyes. You do not come after others and you do not stand at the end of the line when it comes to handing out love. You are first in line to receive from you and you will not be put down by yourself any longer.

When you learn to behave toward yourself with love and kindness and caring, you will be loving number one. You will be taking care of the most important person to you. This is not evil, it is not selfish and it is not wrong. Please love you enough to give to you. This does not mean that you begin to push at everyone else to give to you. If you truly love you, you will not require energy from others. All energy is supplied in full fashion from you and to you. If you are leaking and siphoning off your own energy to others, it is your job to find out how you are losing energy. When you find that it is due to a lack of self-love, you will begin to love you and stop treating you like you don't matter. You are playing a martyr role in some cases, and you are giving away all of your time and energy to others because you do not believe that you deserve it.

You will find that you are not only "not in you" when you siphon all of you off to others; you are also not in love with you. The greater your "need" to assist and give to others, the greater your "need" is to assist and give to yourself. It is a mirror. You teach what you most want to learn and you give what you most want to receive. If you give out big chunks of you, it could be an indication that you really do not like you and are trying to give you away. If you do not give anything and sit and hoard your energy, it could be the same thing. You really don't want to be you so you are suppressing you. It is the same cause in a way. One way is to give you away to get rid of you; the other is to stifle you to get rid of you. In both cases what you require is balance. It is okay to give, and it is okay to keep for yourself or receive. Do not go way out in either direction or you create big problems for yourself.

When you give away your energy it is a good idea to be healthy. If you are not healthy you do not give from a healthy perspective, and then we have all this unhealthy energy running around the planet and it makes everyone it touches a little unhealthy. We must get you well and we must get you to heal your own wounds. Many of you are trying so desperately to heal or fix everyone else, because you have a "big need" to fix your own self. Do not fix them, fix you. Do not heal them, heal you. You will find that once you have healed yourself, you will have assisted the entire world in its healing and its evolution.

Do not be so ready to give you away, and do not be so ready to be the one who is last when it comes to your own energy. Feed you and nurture you. Do not depend on others to do this for you. You are your own source and you are giving to you, you do not command or expect others to give to you. You are the one who nurtures you with your own light. If you must turn to others to receive light then you need to fix you and learn to love you. It is as simple as that. Love is light. Light feeds and nurtures. You have been feeding off of one another for light. Now you are going to learn to turn on your own love light.

You will begin to see the patterns of your life emerge as you begin to see how others react and respond to you. You are at present competing with your own self in an effort to be right, or to get attention, or to get energy. When you see others who are seeking attention it is to show you how you are doing this also. You will see how you have always sought to be "better" in order to win, or to get a pat on the back, or maybe just approval. You are always taught to win and do the best so you can have top billing. Now you all compete and you rate yourselves on a scale for top billing. If you have a good job and a good car you are "good." If you have a lower-level job and a lower-level car you are "not so good."

You will find that as you learn to let go of this system of ratings for one another you will feel much better. You also rate on spiritual goodness. One may be top of the ratings list for preaching and teaching religion, but if you have no religion you may sink to the bottom of the list. High morals rate a high-ranking and low morals rate a low rating. This is how you judge one another, and it is how you have learned to determine who is right for you and who is what you call "wrong" for you. I will let you keep this rating system for now, but I want you to know that it is going to disappear when love takes over. You will no longer feel the need to divide into groups, but this is way in the future. Right now you still feel safe within the confines of your own tribe or group system.

When you go outside of the group, you sometimes upset the balance of the group and they may resent it. You will find that most group consciousness is limited to what the group can readily accept and handle. When you begin to move outside of the group, you will be leaving a hole or void where the group will now feel emptiness or loss. This then creates a feeling of separation, as you have just separated yourself by becoming independent. When you become independent you may upset those who wish to "hold on to you." This may also upset those who wish to hold you back from moving forward into unknown areas of expansion.

When you move out of the realm and the protection of the group you are on your own until you find a new group. You have all experienced this in many ways. Some have seen it within the family unit and others have seen it within groups at work, and you even experience this phenomenon in a simple move from one town to the next. You leave your group or tribe, and usually you join a new group or tribe. This is group consciousness and it is strongly inbred in you, in that it has been passed down in your subconsciousness since the first tribe gathered together for protection, food and strength. This has worked for you for thousands of years and it also works against you. As with everything it has two sides.

Now; when you begin to separate and sit on the sidelines, you begin to see things a little differently. Some of you begin to no longer care for your rating system, and so you begin to decide for yourself what you feel is "for you" or "not for you." This becomes a choice made away from the influence of pack consciousness, and it may be you following your intuition instead of following the other sheep who are in a great deal of fear and very skittish. When you begin to follow your own intuition you will be headed off on your own. You may feel totally alone in your choices but that does not make your choices wrong. When you begin to see the difference between an intelligent behavior and what is acceptable behavior, you will find that not all that has been programmed into groups or society is intelligent, it may just be old patterns that have not yet been broken. You are seeing a lot of old patterns being broken now, and this is not such a bad thing as you judge it to be.

You will find that when you have let go of your old patterns you will no longer be the old you. You will be in a new space in your own self, and you will see how you may choose any situation at any given time. When you begin to release the programmed behavior from previous lives, you will find that you are a bit confused. You will no longer judge people and situations as bad or awful, and you may end up with someone for a best friend who you would have "judged" as undesirable had you not let go of your old programming and judging.

So now you are letting go of right and wrong, and you are confused about what is good for you and what is not. Everything is good if you are in a position to see the gift in it. You need not receive punishment from anyone as you are no longer in the punishment game. If you see how someone is still into punishment you may simply move away from them. It is not necessary to damage you in any way in order to receive love. You will find that when you learn to move over or out of the way, when someone is expelling venom, you will be doing yourself a service. You also may leave if they are whipping around in their own rage and about to explode. It is all clearing and releasing and you need not be on the receiving end.

When you begin to change your programming and how you see things, you will begin to know how you are not going to put you in harm's way. You will grow to trust you when you see how quickly you move out of harm's way and how nicely you move into peace, joy and understanding of any given situation. When you begin to get this flexible, you will create a great deal more freedom in your life. You will find that you are not only 'not' in the punishment game; you are also not in the teaching-how-to-stop-punishment game. You will let go of your need to reform and change others. You will let them be and you will walk forward in life without trying to change and fix everyone else. This, in itself, will give you a sense of peace. You will no longer be trying to drag everyone else into "awareness" with you. You will be lightening your load and allowing everyone else to do their own thing. That frightens you doesn't it? You are so accustomed to stopping the bad guys that you don't know how to trust in divine order. You will learn, and the more you learn the bigger you will become.

You are letting go of a lot in order to gain a lot more. You are transforming from one way to another. You are moving from ignorance and limitation into expansion and intelligence. You are going from dark to light. You are switching from everything is wrong or bad to everything is good or right. You are becoming what you were meant to become. When you are the "light" of the world you will shed "light" on every aspect of your world.

You are moving into a space within you that will "allow" you to not judge. This is a whole new experience for you! You are accustomed to judging everything and you will not know how to live without your judgment. You are addicted to it and you are stuck in it. When you begin to release your hold on judgment you will find that you are in a position to love without restriction or conditions. This is unconditional love. It is love that *is*. Love that *is*, is pure in nature. It does not require restrictions and it does not require paybacks. You are moving into this love and you will be a little confused by it. Allow it to grow and allow it to be. You are doing well on your path to the light. Everything is right on schedule and everyone is right where they planned to be. All is well!

As you begin to unravel and to remember your purpose for coming to earth, you will begin to see how this time of great change was actually put in place by you. You will begin to see how you created this time of change in order to be free of your past and in order to move forward in your healing of spirit. As you begin to experience yourself on many levels you will begin to see how you do not know who you are. You are out of touch with the rest of you and you are out of touch with what you believe. You do not know what you really believe and that is why you are afraid of you. You are afraid because you (this part of you) do not know what you are doing or how you are creating. You are afraid because you do not feel whole. You are afraid because you do not know the answers but you have millions of questions. You are afraid because you are no longer in the dark and you are afraid because you are moving into the light.

When you begin to be all parts of you, you will begin to see how you are not only being afraid or fearful, you are also being the dark and you are being the light that you are moving into. You are the light! It is all in you. You are the darkness and you are the light. You are evil and you were good. You are the devil and you are God. You are the totality of everything. You are the yin and the yang. You are love and hate. You are everything.

When you begin to uncover your extremes you will feel a bit confused and you will want to be left alone by both extremes. You will be overwhelmed by the opposition or opposing energies. You will find that you will want to shut down or shut out both extremes. You will want to stay neutral and to be in your center. This is a good place to be. You do not go too far "off" in one direction or another. You begin to center by balancing these extremes and by allowing everything to be what it is without trying to change it, or to kill it, or to stuff it, or to silence it. You are no longer afraid of extremes when you can allow them to exist without feeling that you must change or fix what is occurring.

When you learn to allow extremes and do not judge them you will begin to see how you are not only coming into balance, you are also going between your extremes in order to achieve balance. You are creating your own teeter-totter effect so that you might learn how to ride in the center and stay calm. You do not go way up and you do not go way down. Part of your fun for many lifetimes has been the thrill of the ups and downs. It is what you like. It is your roller coaster ride. Without the big dips and rises it is an even ride on a straight track. You may not like it. You may find the center very boring and you may wish for the big ups and downs you once knew.

As you begin to come into balance with your extremes you may want to watch for those extremes that have caused pain in the past. Part of the reason you were coming into balance is to let go of pain so that you might embrace pleasure. Pleasure is not always excitement. Pleasure is sometimes very peaceful. Can you handle peace? Do you want pleasure or do you want excitement? Excitement has been very high on your list of priorities for a very long time. Once you let go of excitement you may feel let down and like you have stepped down from the throne. You may feel like you have given up some power when you give up excitement. Excitement is not the part of you that brings you joy. Excitement stimulates you to action, and for peace and calm to prevail you need to slow down and have a little less action.

As you begin to move through your own pain I wish you to remember that you are not creating a new world out of pain. You are releasing old pain and it may cause you to think "Oh no! Not this again. I may never change and have a better life." When you begin to feel as though you are stuck in your programming it is the repeated cycles coming to the surface for you. You need not worry that you will never change and grow out of your patterns. Part of the reason you are feeling pain is to grow "beyond" the pain.

When you learn that you are just clearing and no longer creating new pain, you will begin to see how you are actually receiving a gift. You are looking at pain in order to see what you are, and to change what you are into what you wish to be. In the future you will not be so full of pain as you are now, because you are now bringing your pain to the surface. You have read enough to trigger big changes within you and your subconscious is reacting to the stimulation of new thought created by taken-in new information. As you begin to take on more light you will also take on more awareness. Once you learn to recognize your own awareness, you will have the ability to see clearly what is occurring in any given situation.

As you begin to know you a little better, you will begin to see how you no longer wish to be confused and outside of your own self. Part of bringing you back into you has been to replace programming (that is going) with spirit (that is staying). You are changing one for another.

You are transforming and becoming more of you. You are God and God is now entering you. You invited him in and now he is coming. You are the Second Coming. God is arriving in matter in anyone who is willing to receive him. God does not bust in doors to get received. He is invited then he begins to enter in a very gradual process known as insemination. God is arriving and impregnating you with love. You are being born in love. This is not how you thought you would go to heaven but you will enjoy the end result. As you begin to know your own ability to take on light, you will begin to feel the effects of this type of saturation. You will begin to become aware of certain parts of you that are changing and beginning to stay calm. As you see parts that are calm you will be reassured that this work has only just begun. When you are totally calm and at peace you will have reached your goal of "peace on earth."

As you begin to see how you are connected to everything that occurs in your life, I wish you to remember that you are creator and creation. You start the flow and then you "receive" the flow. When you begin to receive good stuff, no matter what is going on in the rest of the world, you will know that you are delivering your good and you have let go of bad. You will see all as a gift and wonder how you can be so lucky. Each thing that occurs will end up being a gift. It may have caused you concern until you saw the gift, but the trust will be running so strongly in you that the gift in the entire situation will soon be obvious.

As you learn to gracefully receive these gifts you will begin to see how all good flows in the same pattern. It will repeat itself and you will receive more of the same.

When you have received all that you require, you simply step back out of the flow and allow it to pass you by. You need not overstuff yourself, because you know that the flow will always come back to you when you are ready. You, as you recall, are the beginning and the end. You are all things and therefore you have all things. Once you allow the flow to move freely through your life you will be allowing God to move freely through your life. You are God; therefore, you will be allowing all of you into you. You will be accepting all of you, and you will be making you your own best friend by sharing you with you. You will have you back. You will no longer feel like something is missing from your life because you will have returned in full force.

So, as you begin to return you will stir up old programming that has been running the show while you were away. You will find that you are not only no longer in need of this programming, but that this programming is dead and outdated. You will gladly replace it and to do that it must come up and out of you. You will feel it come up to the surface and you will not be comfortable with it. It is leaving so do not worry that it is part of your new life. It is the old stuff hitting the road and leaving you for good. When you begin to see the old stuff come to the surface be sure to say "goodbye" and thank it for whatever it has done in the way of service to you. You are dismissing it, but that does not mean that it has not served you well in the past for whatever your need for it was. It is part of you and you may treat it as such and let it know that it is simply being replaced by God. This outdated part will understand and may even assist you in the replacement process. No one gets left out. All parts have a purpose and all energy can be used and reused.

So, as you allow change and transformation, allow it to be as big and as expansive as you can. Know all of you by communicating with all of you. Allow all parts to know that you are not pushing any parts out; you are simply cleaning up and rearranging your life so that it will flow with the source and not against the source.

When you begin to see how you do not wish to change in certain areas, you will begin to know where you want to be. The things you wish to keep are also the things you wish to be. When you decide what you want to be, you will be deciding how to create you. You will be taking a hand in the creation of your own future and how you will be perceived in it. When you learn to let go of the things you no longer care for, you will be allowing your own self to be more loving. When you carry what you do not care for, you get all grumpy and easily upset. So, the plan is to get you to carry only what you really want. This enables you to be the one who gets to "know thy self" through a process of elimination. You may eliminate whatever is weighing you down and you may lighten your load and only carry love if you can go that far.

As you begin to learn what you want to keep and what you no longer care to keep, you might keep in mind that you are all that there is. You are the whole (totality) of you. You get to mold and shape you and you even get to be the one who calls on you for support once you are molded and shaped. It is as though you create your legs and then you get to walk on them. This is what is taking place. You are creating you. You are learning to be all that you can be in order to use you more efficiently. Once you get you together and whole, you will be able to use all parts of you to create your life. Up until now you have created from limited consciousness. Now you have expanded your consciousness or your perspective, which allows you to be bigger and receive more of creation. As you receive more of creation, you also receive more of you and unload the stuff that blocks more of you from coming into you. You are growing and gaining intensity while you are losing old stuff and letting go of old stuff. Old stuff is pain, hurt, judgment, fear, etc.

So; as you continue to grow and to learn to be what you want, or to change into what is more conducive to your spiritual as well as physical and mental needs, you will find that you are still in the process of "becoming." You are coming into you. Consciousness is entering matter. It is not that you were totally unconscious, but pretty close. Look how much you have gained just by reading this material. As consciousness comes more and more into matter, you will begin to feel a presence fill you. This will be you filling you. You will be "becoming you." You will be growing into you. You are becoming God. This is the

Second Coming and you and your creator are one. You are your creator and you are becoming all that you can be. When you have no more use for expansion, you will begin to contract and take everything back down to your first thought which created it all. That thought was and is "who am I" or "what am I?" It is still being asked and it is still being questioned by you. You do not know "consciously" who or what you are. You are learning about you as you grow.

Pretend you are a seed and you are growing into a plant. You sprout roots and a stem. First you were a tiny seed. The next thing you know you have extremities sticking out of you. You have sprouted. Then you begin to bloom and your whole perception of what you are begins to change again. So we go from tiny round or oval seed to sprouting seed to flowering plant. Then the blooms open and create huge flowers. You have just sprung into something that is big and beautiful! Now you must wait while you look pretty and allow everyone to see your flowers and smell them and touch them. Then you die. Only you do not! Next spring you are right back again creating more beautiful colors. So; who or what are you? Are you the seed, or the roots, or the stem, or are you the beautiful flower? You are *all* things and you constantly change and grow into something new. You are the growth and you are the cycle of growth. You are the creation and you are the cycle that created it.

As you begin to take in more and more of you, you will discover more and more of you. You have a lot to you and you have a lot to learn about you. You may never know all of you but at least you may discover parts of you and learn to love those parts. As you go through your day please remember how magnificent you are. I say this to you because I know how you "forget" from moment to moment who you are. You are God!

When you begin to see how you are simply releasing and clearing your past you will begin to know more about your life. You have never before thought about your life. You take certain things for granted and you do not try to understand how certain things have affected your life. You are learning now to look at the whole picture and to know the whole truth. You are also learning to accept these new, uncovered parts and to assimilate them for your future needs. When you have processed enough of your own insight into your own behavior, you will be allowing you to grow beyond your past behavioral patterns. This will be done by the process of forgiveness. Forgiveness heals all of you and allows all of you to be acceptable. You then begin to integrate and to fall into a new state of being.

As you begin to change all parts of you, you also begin to receive from all of these changed and healed parts. Every part will begin to function at top capacity once it has become healed. You are no longer part of sickness, as you are switching over to wellness. Wellness is part of your natural state of being and wellness is also part of you. You are life; you only pretend to be death. You are love; you only pretend to be fear. You are the light; you only play at being dark.

Once you come back into balance you will find that you no longer have certain needs. Your need for fear will decrease drastically, and you will spend more time in your own state of love. As you begin to see how you are not being free by choosing fear, you will more and more often choose love. Fear will no longer control you. You will be in the position to choose consciously what you experience in life. You will no longer be led around by fear. You will be the one who has regained free will; by choosing to allow God into your life you have allowed freedom back into your life. When you begin to release your right to hold on to things, you will be allowing God to hand you a lifeline. God will allow you to work within certain parameters within your world. As you seek to regain control back from fear, you will be in a position to regain your own lost identity. This is love. You have always been love and you may someday require that you return to your true state. For some of you that day is now. For others, you will wish to come back to love in the very near future.

When you begin to release your hold on who you are and how you want things to be, you will truly be allowing God to take over. You will have come back to God in a very big way. So, as you see change take place *allow* it to be. Do not get upset and do not try to force everything to be as you think it should be. Allow yourself to be free of restrictions so that God might give you your 'good.' You will not always know your 'good' when it arrives, as you are so *programmed* with expectations and bold paradigms. You must learn to receive. You are so busy protecting yourself that you do not know how to receive. This even blocks you from receiving God!

As your fears begin to subside and you begin to walk in trust, you will find that you begin to see the world and those in it from a whole new perspective. You begin to build a new consciousness which will allow you to penetrate your own barriers or taboos. Your walls of protection begin to crumble and you become vulnerable and you become pliable. I know that you have been taught to keep your guard up and to protect you at any cost, but you will find that it is not necessary. In a safe world you do not require walls or protection. You are creating a safe world within you, and soon you will find that your surroundings are reflecting the safeness that is within. You will no longer harm you because you will no longer be judging you as bad. You will only judge you as good and then you will only receive good from you. You are your creator and you are creating everything that occurs in your world.

As you begin to see your world change to a more peace-filled loving world you will begin to see how you are not only being transformed, you are transforming the world you see. You are changing how you view life, and reality, and the world, and in changing your view you change what is viewed. You literally create a whole new perspective, and you do not lose when you begin to receive all perspectives instead of just one... the fear one.

So; as you begin to change how you view any given situation, you will begin to see how you are no longer being led around by "fear of doing the wrong thing." You will know that all choices are simply choices and all possibilities become yours when you allow yourself all those choices. Once you begin to disallow choice you begin to slow down the flow of free will to you. You begin to cut up free will into tiny pieces and say, "No, this is not good" and "No, this is not right" and "No, this is what I did wrong before and I promised I would never do it again." You get yourself all boxed in and you get yourself all caught up in strings of wrong and right, and you spend the rest of your life struggling within you about what is good and what is bad. You may make anything *appear* to be evil and I will come along and show you the gift in it. Learn to see the gifts my friend, it is time to look to the light and let go of looking for the dark.

You are moving very quickly in your assimilation of energy and you are expanding consciousness on a daily basis. You have become so broad that you are twice what you were before you began to read these books. You have literally grown with every word and you are beginning to take on light in areas that have been dark for a very long time. As you have expanded these areas, you have literally allowed light to touch you and in allowing the light to touch you, you have allowed God to touch you and your life. It will not be long before you merge with the light. God is entering and with God you will see your life unfold with beauty and grace. Life is meant to be enjoyed and you have the ability to touch every moment of every day with pure joy. Grace and beauty are yours and you will learn more about them in our next book titled *I and God Are One*. Know that you are in touch with God and know that God is touching you.

In addition to writing these books for God I also communicate with God on a more personal level each day. This is one of my personal writings that I thought you might enjoy….

*Y*ou will soon begin to enter a phase in your evolution that will assist you in your times of need. This phase will be trust. Trust will allow you to move more freely and trust will allow you the insight you require in any given situation. All situations are presented with wisdom. You do not necessarily know who or what you are evolving into but you will eventually see. It is like a butterfly who is being born. The caterpillar may be very upset about the loss of all those legs but a butterfly simply does not require them. You will find that changes will occur within your reality that you do not understand, and when they do I want you to remember that you are becoming a butterfly. Nothing will be the same and your old rules will have to be left behind in your old world. You can fly now and it is no longer necessary to carry all the old rules that kept the caterpillar alive and well. The new rules apply to wings and brilliant shades of colors that are flitting from this flower to that plant. Your old body would not flit, it could only crawl and it certainly required a lot of feet on the ground.

Now you do not require all those feet on the ground. You do not require all those legs and you will never again return to caterpillar status. Once transformed you are forever transformed. Once you have flown, you will never wish to be grounded again. It may take a little getting used to in the beginning, but you will enjoy not having all those feet and all those legs. Let go and fly with enthusiasm into your new self. Know that you are being guided and there is no wrong way. Know that every part of you is evolving and you are afraid because you are losing parts. It is okay to lose parts and to become new. It is okay to be you. It is okay to fly and to lose all those legs. You don't need them. Trust will get you into the air and trust will assist you in letting go of unnecessary beliefs, attitudes, behaviors and ideas. Let trust guide you and you will be in "love." Trust and love are part of one another and they do not exist alone. You each have trust and you each have love. Love is all and trust is part of love. You will find that the most efficient way to transform is to "love" and "trust" your own self. You are being guided and you are not alone.

You will be very happy to know that not only do you require no air to breathe you also require no food to eat. You only believe you require these and so you have created these needs. In the overall scheme of things you cannot pollute the air and you cannot poison your food supply. You, however, have not arrived at your advanced state of understanding such complexities. When you begin to see how it is impossible to kill off the earth, or anything else, you will be very surprised. You will also be very surprised to know that you do not actually begin to know your own God-self until you learn to accept your own God-self as you. You have a great deal of work to do so I suggest you begin by allowing everything to "be." It is not necessary to judge what you create as undesirable. Just when you start complaining about what you are losing (your legs) you will begin to see what you are gaining (your brilliant new wings).

God's Pen

I first heard the voice of God in 1988. I was sitting in my back yard reading a book when this big booming voice interrupted with, "I am God and I will not come to you by any other name." I felt like the voice was everywhere – inside of me as well as in the sky around me. I was so frightened that I ran in my bedroom to hide.

This was not the first time that I heard voices. I had been communicating with my own spirit guide or soul for about a year. I guess my depth of fear regarding God, and all that he represented to me at the time, was just too much.

I spent two days trying to avoid the voice of God, which was patiently waiting for me to respond. By the second day I was exhausted from lack of sleep and decided to give in and talk with him. This turned out to be the greatest gift and best decision of my life.

The first book, *God Spoke through Me to Tell You to Speak to Him*, shows my evolution from communicating with my soul to communicating with the Big Guy. It took a couple years for me to be comfortable communicating with God. My fear of a punishing God was big! That has most definitely changed and I now think of God as my partner and best friend.

In the beginning the voice of God would wake me in the middle of the night and tell me it was time to write. He said I had promised to do this work (I assumed he was talking about the soul/spirit me). I would drag myself up to a sitting position and watch in amazement as my hand flew across the page, while I tried to keep up by reading what was being written.

It was always so much fun to wake up the next morning and grab my notebook to see what God had written during the night. After some time the voice stopped waking me and I became comfortable picking up my pen and writing for God first thing in the morning. I think in the beginning I had to be awakened while still semi-conscious from sleep so I wouldn't object too much to the information that was being channeled through me.

As I grew less and less afraid (and more trusting) of God, he was able to communicate greater information. Some of the information is quit controversial, but I felt it important to just let it be and not censor it. I present the writings here to you as they were given to me. I have edited a little (mostly the more personal information regarding myself) and I have used a pen name for privacy reasons. I asked God for a good pen name and he guided me to Liane which (I was told) in Hebrew means "God has answered."

At one point I became a little concerned about my sanity in all this, so I went to a hypnotherapist to find out what I was doing. Under hypnosis I saw this incredibly huge beam of light with a voice coming from within it. It was a giant "loving light" and felt so comforting and kind. It felt like that's where I came from. After that I stopped worrying about my sanity. If this is crazy, I think it's a very good kind of crazy to be….

In loving light, Liane

Loving Light Books

Available at:
Loving Light Books: www.lovinglightbooks.com
Amazon: www.amazon.com
Barnes & Noble: www.barnesandnoble.com

Also Available on Request at Local Bookstores

www.ingramcontent.com/pod-product-compliance
Lightning Source LLC
Chambersburg PA
CBHW031844090426
42741CB00005B/350

9781878480156